Hurry Up Nurse!

DAWN BROOKES

To Judith

Happy Memories

Love
Alan

D1513152

Hurry Up Nurse!

Memoirs of nurse training in the 1970's

By

DAWN BROOKES

DAWN BROOKES PUBLISHING

This book is a work of non-fiction based on the author's experiences. In order to protect privacy, names, identifying factors, dialogue and details have been changed or reconstructed.

Published by DAWN BROOKES PUBLISHING
www.dawnbrookespublishing.com

Paperback Edition 2016
ISBN: 978-0-9955561-0-2

Cover Design by Janet Dado
Printed and bound in Great Britain by Biddles Books Ltd

To Gail for pointing me in the right direction

Preface

This book includes a collection of memories from my experiences of nurse training during the 1970's and early 1980's. I trained as both a State Enrolled Nurse and a Registered General Nurse during these years. I have deliberately intermingled stories from both sets of training as they were both very similar apart from the assessments which are not the subject of this book. The training undertaken, occurred in and around Leicester and Berkshire. The majority of experiences shared occurred between 1977 and 1980.

The procedures and practices outlined throughout this book are a true recollection of my memories of them as are the antics of myself and fellow students and doctors. I loved my training (both times) although obviously there were some trying times that will be shared in this book.

It took me quite a while to decide on a title for this work but in the end I decided on *Hurry up Nurse* as this reminded me so much of life on NHS hospital wards. We were always in demand, hurrying from one patient to another as there never seemed to be enough hours in the day. I hope that as well as sharing the hustle and bustle of working in hospitals, I have also managed to portray just how much we cared.

I have tried to recreate the events, localities and conversations from my memory although I have changed the names of individuals and places to protect confidentiality' of patients and anonymity of others. I have also mixed up identifying characteristics to further protect anonymity. I may have changed details of wards and the order of training in some instances.

It is with pride that I present this book to the reader and I hope that it will provide you with an insight into hospital life at the time written about. I am proud of myself and my colleagues for making it through those turbulent years of growing up while coming to terms with the discipline of nurse training. I hope this comes across. I do hope that you enjoy reading the book and you never know there may be more to follow.

Chapter 1

The Interview – 1977

'Why do you want to be a nurse, Miss Brookes?'

'Good question,' I thought but knew I needed a decent answer. 'I would like to help people when they are at their most vulnerable, when they are ill.' I improvised, I couldn't really say. *'A friend told me I should be a nurse because I couldn't think of anything better to do and she wished she had finished her training,'* even though that was nearer the truth. At least I had worked out that nursing involved caring for the sick. That statement and this interview was the beginning of the next thirty-nine years of my life.

The selection process for nursing was an all day affair. I had written an application letter in January of 1977 and was called for interview in April. At the grand age of eighteen, I had never had an interview with more than one person before and it was a bit daunting as there would be three people on the panel, what's worse, I didn't really know why I was there. I had no clue what nursing was all about.

First of all I was shown into a room with a desk which immediately made me feel uncomfortable, reminding me of school days (my latter years at school hadn't gone well). I was a bit nervous but felt quite good as I had dressed in my only decent clothes consisting of a black skirt, white blouse, black jacket and tie, ok the tie bit is made up. After about five minutes a rather serious looking woman came in and introduced herself as Mrs Butcher, thankfully butcher by name not by nature, she was wearing a maroon uniform with a frilly hat, she appeared to be in her fifties with round spectacles and a serious but not unkind demeanour.

'Good morning Miss Brookes, before the interview 'we' need to sit an entrance exam as we do not have the educational qualifications to be interviewed directly, that really boosted my confidence. I was a bit confused as to why she needed to sit the exam too but daren't ask, realising later that 'we' was the royal 'we' used by experienced nurses who often included the 'we' word in their statements and questions.

'How are we today; we are just going to have a little injection; we are going to theatre today for an amputation aren't we?' and so on. Of course, many nurses were not looking for a reply to the questions at all. I bet many a patient wished the 'we' really did mean we. Focus Dawn I told myself as I found myself daydreaming already, this had been my problem at school; there was always something more interesting, hence my reports.

'If Dawn spent as much time studying as she did daydreaming and talking she would do so much better,' had been a recurring theme. If only teachers realised the impact these statements had on my poor longsuffering mother they wouldn't have said such things.

Back to the present, 'After sitting the exam we will have a fifteen minute break and then return to this room.' Mrs Butcher continued, 'If we have passed the exam we will be given an interview.' Next I was given an examination paper and told to start the test which I had forty-five minutes to complete. The test seemed relatively easy to me and was based on IQ ability with mainly English and Maths questions, I sat an almost identical exam again four years later when I decided to become a registered nurse. I didn't meet any other candidates on the day of my interview; I guess they all had the required educational qualifications.

'We' did pass and I was accepted into nurse training, apparently I had done well in the entrance exam but was not told how well, second time around I got ninety eight percent. Because of the result, there was some discussion around whether I should do a two year course to train as a State Enrolled Nurse (SEN) or a three year course to train as a State Registered Nurse (SRN, now renamed Registered General Nurse, RGN); it's hard to keep up. I wasn't sure of the difference nor was I used to studying. I think the interviewers saw my blank expression and agreed that it would be best for me to do the two year training. While this meant that it would ultimately be a longer route to my final destination, it was the right choice as I was not at all studious and enjoyed a very hectic social life. I think I would have fallen at the first hurdle if I had done it the other way round. It is somewhat ironic that I have since spent most of my life studying.

After the interview Mrs Butcher warned me that nursing would be hard work, with long hours, difficult shift patterns including nights, lots of study with little thanks, low pay (very low pay I would have said) and that I would feel tired most of the time. I was almost on my way out of the door when she smiled whimsically and stated.

'However, it is one of the most rewarding jobs in the world and many of your friends will be in jobs they hate but you will be pleased to know that YOU will not be joining them.' I couldn't walk out after that. How true those words were and thereafter followed a thirty-nine year career.

Following this with the lecture over, I was sent off to Occupational Health for a medical examination. I first saw a doctor and then a nurse. The whole thing was a bit too thorough for my liking with a lot of health questions. I was eighteen for goodness sake. I hadn't had time to be ill had I? The doctor did a lot of poking and prodding, listened to my heart and lungs and then the nurse took my blood pressure and tested my urine. The only advice I received, was that my posture was poor and I should stretch my back to stop myself getting a curvature of the spine. That sounded nasty so I said I would try although I'm not sure I ever did try as my posture is still poor. Next I was sent for blood tests.

It was the first time in my life I had to have blood taken and for some reason I asked if the nurse could take it from my right arm as I thought I might faint if she took it from the left. She totally ignored my request.

'Don't be silly.' She retorted and promptly took it from my left arm and yes, I did almost faint. I had to go and sit down for a while afterwards with a glass of water while the nurse glared at me for being such a baby. I apologised for keeping her but inwardly I was yelling at her for not listening to me. I have never allowed anyone to take blood from my left arm since. Totally illogical but it works for me, funnily enough, I always give patients a choice of arm for blood tests now although when I first started training, apart from occupational health nurses, only doctors and medical students were allowed to take blood.

Finally, the most exciting part of the day, I was sent to the sewing room to be measured up for uniforms and by now the news was sinking in and I was feeling pretty ecstatic and so proud of myself. The process had taken up most of the day and I left having been told that if I was successful, I think this meant, if I hadn't got bubonic plague, I would get a letter giving me a start date which was likely to be in September of that year. Wow, what a day.

When the letter finally arrived I was pretty pleased with myself. It meant I was making Brookes' family history being the first person to embark on a professional career as far as I know. My background was very much working class. The majority of my relatives worked in shops, factories or as self employed labourers. My grandparents on my mum's side had been farm labourers. I did have one very successful uncle who had become a self-made millionaire through antique dealing and the last time I had seen him before starting my nurse training, he was driving a white Rolls Royce which did look a bit out of place in our street. He used to hire it out for weddings (ever the businessman), had divorced his first wife, leaving her and the four children for a much younger model and now lived in a huge house in a posh part of Leicester, I was told he had a swimming pool. Women in the family mostly married and had children although many of them worked as well, there were a few shirkers who preferred to live off the State.

One of my aunts had a market stall and sold clothes, I remember as a child I had occasionally gone with my mum on a Saturday to help out on the stall.

'BEST JUMPERS, BLOUSES AND SKIRTS!' my aunt would shout to passers' by, as I cringed with embarrassment. The market was fun though and always a hive of activity with traders shouting out all day long trying to sell their wares. I quite enjoyed those Saturdays and although they were often cold and long, I always got pop (fizzy drinks) and crisps to keep me happy. The smell of the fruit, vegetables and fish stalls is forever etched on my memory.

The events I didn't enjoy were the jumble sales, mostly replaced now by car boot sales. Weekly jumble sales held in church halls that my aunt would attend to buy nearly new stuff to add to her stock and my mum would go in order to buy me and my brother clothes. There was always a queue outside the door as eager parents and grannies would be ready to get the first bargain. The doors would open and me and my brother would be carried along in the throng before being pushed to the back as people from behind used any means possible to get to the front.

Jumble sales were dangerous places for children but we would bravely find our way to the toy stall to see if we could buy anything for a penny and sometimes we did.

'How much is this?' I once asked as I found a prized Beano annual,

'A penny,' the lady replied, even though I later noticed it was marked tuppence (2d pre-decimalisation). I think she had seen the penny in my hand, I was over the moon.

'Come here Dawn and help me with these.' My aunt shouted, I couldn't see her for the melee, but suddenly a pile of clothes appeared with my aunt underneath them and we put them into bags, all the time I was hugging my Beano annual close to my chest. My brother had found himself a Victor Annual so he was happy and my mum had found us our clothes. Almost a great success then except I was always a bit embarrassed about wearing clothes from a jumble sale, this probably wasn't helped by school friends taunting at school.

'Where did you get those clothes, at a 'rummage' sale? Dawn's mam can't afford new clothes.' When I first heard Dolly Parton's 'Coat of Many Colours' song it reminded me of those days and although it was difficult at the time, I now look back proudly at how my mum dressed us through hard times. She did a lot of knitting too and we did always have new jumpers.

My family roots reminded me of a joke where a man complained:

'I preferred the good old days when women married, stayed home, looked after children and did the washing, cooking, cleaning and ironing. Now,' he said 'women marry have children, go to work, come home and *THEN* do the washing cooking, cleaning and ironing.' Not much has changed.

My mum and many of my aunts also did this. Many working class women, those that are benefits shy rather than work shy have rarely had the opportunity to stay home and look after children. My dad, however, was another story; he hardly ever held down an honest job for very long, not that he stayed home to look after the children as he was always looking for a get rich quick scheme. My brother and I have always joked that he only ever worked for about four weeks in the whole of his life. This of course is an exaggeration but I don't think we were too far off the mark.

My mum was the complete opposite, a more honest and hard working woman would be difficult to find and she always held down a job, refusing to ask the State for anything, even though there were times when she would have been entitled to do so. I think the only thing we had due to being poor was free school meals. It would seem that both my brother and I inherited our mum's work ethic and we have worked hard since leaving school, a fact of which the State should be very proud. I do think there should be rewards for a good work ethic, perhaps I'll find myself on the Honours list someday – that's if the Prime Minister reads this book which is unlikely as I am not anticipating a 'best seller'.

The acceptance letter explained that I had been accepted as a pupil nurse on a two year training course and training would consist of working in any or all of the three hospitals in Leicester:

- The Leicester Royal Infirmary
- Groby Road Hospital
- The Leicester General Hospital

I would be attending Charles Frears School of Nursing for theory and practical training in between working on the wards and was to report there at nine o clock in the morning on the set date. There was a list of things to buy prior to starting. I was excited and couldn't wait until September.

1977 was a very eventful year, not just because of me beginning my nursing career but also because of other landmark occasions; Queen Elizabeth II's Silver Jubilee was one, I remember the nationwide street parties including the one I went to in Leicester, it seemed such a happy time that brought strangers together with a sense of national pride and joy. Just before that party my best friend Cheryl and I had met a rather odd couple who stand out in my memory for chanting in very loud voices.

'WE KNOW WHERE YOU'RE GOING!' Every time someone went to the toilet, the bizarre things that become memories. Virginia Wade won the women's Singles final at Wimbledon in front of the Queen which seemed rather apt. It was also the year the first Star Wars film was launched (who would have believed that the films would become so iconic) and the tragic death of Elvis Presley, aged 42, who I had idolised for as long as I could remember.

I was at home with my mum watching TV when the newscaster appeared on screen and announced:

'We interrupt this programme to bring you a newsflash, Elvis Presley is dead.' I don't remember the rest, I was crying, I couldn't believe it was true, there were floral tributes at Graceland and a great outpouring of public grief (perhaps that's where public mourning began). The next day's newspapers confirmed the truth of the event and for weeks there were lots of tributes and discussions about what had caused his death. Rumours of drugs soon emerged and the rest, as they say, is history. The most exciting part of 1977 for me of course was that life changing interview.

Chapter 2

Nurse Training - Back to School

I really did go back to school; it was called PTS (Pupil Training School). I was very excited on the first day although a bit nervous as I got the two buses to Charles Frears School of Nursing, even the name sounded special. The beautiful building of Charles Frears has recently been sold by De Montfort University, Leicester. I entered it for the final time in June 2010 for yet another interview, this time to apply to do a doctorate in health sciences. It was a poignant moment for me as the building was very soon to be closed. After the interview I crossed the road and saw the house where I lived in a bedsit during my second year of training, memories of living there will be shared later in this book.

Upon arrival at the building back in 1977, I was ushered into a classroom full of excited girls, mostly my age. I found an empty desk and sat at it and began chatting to the group around me.

'Where have you come from?' Said the girl on my left, she was taller than me with curly brown hair and freckles,

'I live in Leicester.' I replied, 'What about you?'

'I'm from Manchester, I moved into the nursing home on Saturday, this is Grace from London,' she said as she turned her head to the girl on her left who had blonde hair and was very pretty, 'and I am

Sue.' We exchanged hellos and spent the next few minutes sharing experiences. They had both left home and moved into the nursing home which was divided into flats with four people sharing. Two other girls they were sharing with were pointed out, sitting at the back of the class. 'That's Charlie with the dark hair and glasses and that's Bette wearing the jeans.' Sue explained.

They were looking forward to the next few years and had already found the local nurses' pub. I felt fractionally jealous as I was back living at home with mum and brother while these girls were going to be having the time of their lives in a nursing home. I did share nursing home life a few years later in London.

'I can't wait to get to know the handsome doctors.' Grace laughed and true to her word she did get to know quite a few and Sue and I would be picking up the pieces as she fell in and out of love over the next few years. The hubbub stopped as Mrs Butcher walked in the room and stood at the front of the class.

'Good morning, girls.' She said The Prime of Miss Jean Brodie came to mind but no Scottish accent. 'Welcome to Leicester and Charles Frears, my name is Mrs Butcher, I met most of you at interview and I will be your classroom tutor throughout your training over the next few years. This week is the introductory week and I will let you have a timetable in a minute.'

The 'in a minute', so reminded me of an experience of being a hospital inpatient when I was a child. I was eight years old and one night I woke up with terrible pain in my side, I crawled downstairs to get a drink of water, my mum heard me, she got up and realised I was in a lot of pain and sat with me for a while. The pain didn't go away so she put on her coat and said she was going to call an ambulance, it was around three o clock in the morning and we didn't have a home phone so she had to walk to the end of the road in the middle of the night to the public telephone box and call the ambulance, not that I gave that a thought at the time. When the ambulance came I remember the men trying to cheer me up by telling me that I was special and they were going to set off the flashing blue light to get me to hospital, I was pleased about this and managed a smile, they didn't use the siren though because they didn't want to wake people up.

Once in hospital I was seen by doctors who examined my abdomen a bit and I was admitted into a bed on a children's ward, my mum was sent home, perhaps as well as my brother was still in bed. I couldn't sleep as the pain was gripping me and the doctors had decided it probably wasn't appendicitis so they allowed me to drink. A kind nurse came.

'Can't you sleep?' she asked,

'No.' I replied,

'Would you like a glass of milk?'

'Yes please.' I loved milk.

'I'll be back in a minute,' she said and that was the last I saw of her. I waited and waited, in the end fighting sleep because I thought she would be back with my milk at any moment. Eventually I drifted off and when I woke in the morning there was no glass of milk by my bed.

Later that day I was asked to turn on my side while the nurse put something up my bottom (I now know it was a suppository), I had no idea what she was doing but obeyed as a child would. The nurse then said I had to wait in bed until she came back and that she would be back 'in a minute'. I waited and waited again and began to feel desperate for the toilet but I daren't get out of bed in case I got into trouble. The abdominal cramps got worse and worse and I was sitting on my bottom, sweating and feeling terrible, terrified that I might mess the bed and yet frightened of getting out as I had been told to wait. Finally I knew I could wait no longer and decided to risk a dash to the toilet which I found quickly to great relief. When I got back to bed my mum was there, I ran to her and cried. The nurse came and asked if I had been to the toilet, I nodded, frightened she would tell me off and she gave a big smile and said I could go home. I was so relieved in more ways than one.

As I remembered those events in that moment I made a deal with myself and to future patients everywhere that my 'in a minute' would mean just that and I would never allow myself to forget to go back even if the minute did stretch a little and as far as I am aware I have kept that deal although I guess I might not remember if I forgot. Not a great start though, I had only been in the classroom a few minutes and I was already daydreaming.

'Today is the first day of your nursing career,'

Mrs Butcher continued, 'and I see that some of you are already getting to know each other,' she glared at a group of three girls chatting at the back, one of them was Bette, the flatmate of my new found friends, who immediately stopped talking while going red in the face.

We would get to know that glare very well, Mrs Butcher was a kind lady but she also carried an air of authority and only had to look, to command obedience which must have come from her years working as a ward sister. 'Shortly, I will split you into two groups as there are forty-six of you altogether and you will be shown around the building. Before the end of your training I am afraid at least ten of you will give up, some of you will be asked to leave and another ten of you will fail finals.' We looked a bit stunned and I glanced around the class to see which ones were the likely drop out candidates and noticed a few others were doing the same thing. I didn't dare look for the failures and as for being asked to leave that didn't bear thinking about.

That day we were shown around the School of Nursing that was Charles Frears, there were a few classrooms with desks, Clinical rooms with beds and odd looking equipment, a canteen and various administration offices. Mid afternoon we were given our whole training timetable, this included the type of ward placement with dates and the School blocks and holidays. It was the most exciting part of the day and I treasured that timetable for years to come.

During the first week we had to open a bank

account in order to be paid, pay was going to be monthly, I had been used to cash in an envelope on a Friday. Most of us opened accounts with a well known major bank as they came on-site to encourage us to sign up, a good ploy as I have been with the same bank ever since. A few weeks later I received a cheque book and a cheque guarantee card; I felt really grown up now but didn't know how to get money out of the bank. My mum didn't get paid into a bank either so she couldn't help. Before the development of multiple 'hole in the wall' cash machines I used to write out a cheque to myself and take it into the bank to exchange for cash. An early cash machine appeared outside the main branch of St. Martin's in the town centre and I got to use that regularly. I was recently in that part of Leicester and noticed, that too had closed and was no longer a bank.

I was permanently overdrawn for approximately ten years until I finally adapted to living on my low salary. While I was doing my RGN training I would work as an agency nurse on my days off to supplement my income, often working seven days a week, I did this throughout my training and even after qualifying for some years until my salary increased.

We were trained mainly on the wards, learning our theory in two week blocks interspersed with eight to ten week ward placements. The Briggs report from 1972 was implemented following a change of law in 1979 and from then on nurse training became less focussed on the medical model and more on psychology and sociology, with the nursing process being adopted from the USA. This was followed later with Project 2000 where nurses were trained at diploma and degree level. Just a few years ago Nursing and midwifery Council declared that this nurse training was not fit for purpose. My training wasn't perfect but somehow the experiences gained during training helped us to deal with the challenges following qualification a little better I think than many trained under the new systems.

During those first few weeks I became friends with quite a few of the girls in my set and we had a few nights out but we were never a group that gelled closely together to keep in touch for years to come although we did gel in smaller groups. Most of us concentrated on getting through the training and qualifying.

Anatomy and physiology was hard work for most of us who had not paid enough attention to human biology at school. We were taught every human system starting with the skeletal system. At first the novelty helped me to concentrate but it was hard going for someone who didn't like sitting in a classroom. The saving factor was that we were all in it together and we would chivvy each other along and when one of us seemed to be struggling, the others would get around us and help.

We also had practical sessions which helped break up the days. Bed making was one of the first things we were taught in the practical rooms, not exactly vital to life but it was a start. We had to place two chairs at the foot of the bed and we would fold back the bedding over these chairs. Two of us would stand either side of the bed and we were taught how to strip a bed without filling the room with dust and then how to remake a bed using hospital corners. It's sad I know, but I had been dying to learn how to do hospital corners as I had heard about them from a friend. Once learnt never forgot, I was to make thousands of beds in my career and the novelty soon wore off.

It was always fun in the practical room; we could let our hair down a bit and play practical jokes on each other when Mrs Butcher wasn't looking.

We were taught how to feed a patient and give drinks without choking them; this was actually much more difficult on the wards. Some of this we practised on each other which was always fun; trying to give each other drinks from plastic beakers with a spout was, at times hilarious. At first we took it all very seriously but soon started messing around and instead of being gentle, offering sips we would try to pour the whole drink down our pretend patient's throat until they spluttered and spat it out. Mrs Butcher would usually allow a little bit of messing and then calm us down in an instant with one of those looks. Bed bathing was taught on a life sized Manikin doll, I don't think we were up to washing each other, not sure whether that would have been too embarrassing or too dangerous. The Manikins did have to suffer an awful lot in our hands over the years as we were taught to pass naso-gastric tubes, put in urinary catheters, and give enemas and so on.

As I said, the anatomy and physiology sessions were hard going but absolutely necessary to understand what was going on with patients once we were on the wards.

We were introduced to the wards with a few visits prior to starting our first placements. Getting used to the odours from antiseptics and disinfectants that were used to cover those of excrement and bodily discharges was something that would take some time to nurture. During the first eight weeks of training which was mostly classroom based, we took a trip to one of the wards with a Clinical Tutor. The first thing that struck me was the smell of hospital, (in later years I visited a Children's hospital in Romania shortly after the revolution and execution of the Ceausescu's, and I didn't know it when I started, but our hospitals smelt like palaces in comparison. All the photos in the world could not portray a smell that could only be experienced, I did take photos in the Romanian hospital and it was awful but the smell of anaerobic bacteria from rotting flesh was one never to be forgotten, I can smell it as I write now.

We were escorted behind curtains to be taught how to give a bed bath to a real patient. I can never forget the poor elderly lady lying in the bed, barely conscious, nor the smell of bodily fluids mixed with the heat. It took every ounce of energy and concentration for me not to pass out. I had visions of myself being put into the bed next to the patient which tended to focus the attention somewhat. The

Clinical Tutor, totally oblivious, treated the patient with the utmost respect, explaining to her throughout while teaching us, she continued with her bed bath demonstration and must have thought I was very attentive with my fixed stare, the reality was, I was trying to hold it together and not let my new friends know I might faint at any minute.

I certainly could not remember a single word she said but I can remember the respect and dignity she showed to that lady and this was something we were taught from the very beginning. That was one of the times I had second thoughts about my chosen career and I really wasn't sure I would ever make it, my first step onto a real ward and I was ready to run. This was not what it was like in books or in one of the popularised TV programmes at the time; 'Emergency Ward 10'. It certainly bore no resemblance to the current Casualty or Holby City. Where were all those glamorous people I ask myself? I did meet some later though as nurses and patients come from all walks of life.

When it came to ward placements we were all split up and sent out into the big wide world of hospital life either by ourselves or in twos. It was always a bit daunting starting a new ward, not knowing anyone and not knowing the routine, occasionally two of us from the set got sent to a new ward and this was always a bonus although usually working opposite shifts. The hospital had a staff canteen and that was where we got to meet up with each other, share food, experiences and more importantly the support that sometimes kept us going. Some wards were easier to settle into than others but the worst times came when you hated a ward and the placement seemed to last for an eternity. There weren't many like this during my training but there were a few, always caused by staff members never by patients. It was when working on these wards that the support from each other became vital as it stopped many of us from walking away from our career.

I think almost every nurse has nearly given up at some time during their training and some did discover that this really wasn't what they wanted to do for the rest of their lives, bringing Mrs Butcher's prediction into grim reality, I think eleven people who began training in our 1977 set left and didn't complete. I think what kept me going was partly remembering where I came from but mainly the fact that I fell in love with the job, I loved the patients and I made some really good friends that I kept in touch with for many years, patients and staff.

Chapter 3

Growing up - Simple Beginnings

I was brought into the world at a quarter past six one morning in the winter of 1959 in a cramped bedsit in Nottingham. My brother, Dave had been born in Lincoln eighteen months earlier. My mum told me she and dad couldn't agree on a name so the midwife intervened,

'Look Mr & Mrs Brookes, as she was born at dawn why don't you call her Dawn?' So that was it I was named Dawn. The only error, I recently found out when tracing my family tree, was that they were not Mr & Mrs Brookes at all. My dad had been previously married, something I never knew and when my mum became pregnant with my brother Dave, she was single which was highly embarrassing for her at the time as it was not yet the swinging sixties but 1957. She had to be shipped off (well, bussed) to The Quarry Maternity Home, a maternity home run by nuns in Lincoln for her confinement and delivery of my brother. This had been arranged by her younger sister, Hazel and her boss who were very supportive. My dad was absent from the event which was not the first time and certainly wouldn't be the last.

The Quarry was mainly occupied by single mothers who put their babies up for adoption and I wonder now, many years later whether that was what my mum was considering at the time, if that had been the case I might never have been born, interesting thought. My poor mother was surrounded by strangers giving birth to her first baby and my brother's birth wasn't registered until six years later and his certificate had to be specially authorised by the Registrar General because of the time lapse, he still smarts over it.

My birth was registered in the normal way though and my dad must have got a divorce as my parents were finally married in the registry office in Nottingham three and a half years later on the quiet, my brother would have been nearly six and he doesn't recall the marriage so they must have snuck off, with witnesses I have never heard of.

We lived in a fairly cramped bedsit in Nottingham until I was about five years old. I have vague memories of the room with a double bed where we all slept and a kitchen down a hallway. I also remember an enormous overgrown garden where me and my brother played and which we called The Jungle, paradise for two young children.

The landlord was a Sikh gentleman surprisingly called Mr Singh and when he kindly offered to take me on holiday with him to India my dad thought it was a good idea. My mum, however, was the more sensible of the two and declined the offer. I have always had doubts about my dad's paternal instinct and this story just confirms them. I'm sure the landlord meant well but what parent would let an under five year old go to India with a relative stranger – answer; 'my dad'.

I think my first introduction to hospitals was an event that is forever ingrained on my mind, my brother and a few friends were out playing. It was a lovely sunny day and we went to play in the local 'woods yard' which was a favourite place of ours, nearby. There was a conveyor belt that carried wood through for shredding and we would jump on the conveyor belt for a ride and then jump off at the end just before it went through to the shredder, more like a crusher really. My brother, Dave missed his footing and was being dragged through the machine screaming his head off; it was terrifying so I ran off to fetch my mum and to get away from the noise. Fortunately, while I was gone the machine operator heard my brother's screams, turned the machine off and called an ambulance. When my mum and I arrived at the scene it was bedlam. My brother was wailing and there was blood everywhere, his leg looked horrible and he ended up in hospital for 3 months with multiple compound fractures to the leg. He was lucky to be alive and we learned the lesson, not to play in the woods yard. The man who worked there was obviously very upset and he took my brother a basket of fruit the next day, I remember eating the grapes as he was feeling a bit queasy.

This wasn't the only major accident encountered in my early life. Next up was my dad, he had being working somewhere with electrics. Heaven only knows why because he was hopeless at DIY, so what maniac let him loose with electrics I will never know. Thankfully there are rules against this now.

Anyway he was badly electrocuted and my rich Uncle Vernon came round to tell my mum. It was all very hush, hush but I heard Vernon say.

'It was his rubber boots that saved him.' I was determined that I would someday get a pair of rubber boots as I might need them to save me one day.

We didn't see my dad for a long time as we were not allowed to go to the hospital because, we were told, it would be too frightening. Nothing is more frightening than a child's imagination though so I think it would have been better if we had been allowed to visit. Finally he was to come home and my uncle said.

'Now don't be shocked when your dad comes.' Spoken in that secretive way in which adults speak to children. Finally, he arrived, the first thing I noticed were his hands covered in scabs and then he came over to me like something out of a horror movie, his face was also covered in scabs.

'Give us a kiss then' He said and I ran away to hide which was probably not the most mature thing to do but I was not going to kiss Frankenstein. My brother and I sat giggling in the nervous way that children do when presented with something shocking (not meant to be a pun). We soon got used to it, although I didn't like to get too close in case any of the scabs would come off or I might catch something, I had read somewhere about leprosy and that if you touched a person with leprosy your limbs would fall off so I wasn't taking any chances.

The electric shock had virtually stripped all of my dad's tattoos from his arms and hands, I never did like those tattoos anyway, and he was left with scars. His face, though, recovered with hardly any trace of the burns in spite of looking like a mummy prior to taking the bandages off. My dad kept photographs which he would take out at the most inopportune moments and show to people, including my school friends, scaring them to death. It was always reassuring to know that he would disappear for a while during my childhood.

We moved to Leicester where my parents originated from and into our first house in 1965. It was a three bedroom council house, I had my own bedroom for the first time in my life, and I was now six. The house had no running hot water and no central heating. The bath was in the kitchen and covered with a big wooden board which was used as a storage shelf. Every Sunday the board would come off and my mum would heat water in saucepans and gradually fill the bath.

We took turns to have a bath, dad first, then mum, then Dave and finally me, the youngest. Obviously the water was filthy and lukewarm by the time I got in but it was still a rare treat. To this day I enjoy a bath all to myself and will spend an hour in there with a good book daily when I get home from work. The toilet was outside and down the yard so it is not surprising that I learned to hold for long periods of time. Mum and dad had a bucket in the bedroom, common at the time; in case they were caught short in the night. I always thought this was disgusting and still remember the wee smell in their bedroom even though my mum tried to disguise it with scent.

We had a coal fire and once we had a chimney fire which was quite exciting as the fire brigade had to be called, this was also a common occurrence, not in our house but in the 1960's. I remember the miners' strikes in the late 1960's and again in 1972 because we were freezing. Our next door neighbour was Mrs Clarke, a widow, who lived on her own with a mongrel dog called Tinker. She was always very nice and I remember she used to bleach the front yard and the path outside her house every weekend.

Dad was away again for about three years while we lived in the house and so it was me, my mum and my brother along with my cat, Timmy and our Poodle, Shandy. Shandy had two litters of puppies that I remember which stands out, seeing the miracle of birth for the first time at the age of six was spectacular. I watched the puppies for hours on end as they fed and developed and could lose myself in this amazing world of nature, much later I became a midwife and that miracle of new life was increased exponentially in my mind.

When one of my uncle's re-married after the death of his first wife much to the disgust of his children we acquired his dog, a boxer, called Prince who would be with us until I was sixteen when he dropped dead in the kitchen which was a frightening experience.

Prince often used to collapse but get up again

and on this occasion I was getting dinner ready for when mum got home from work, Dave was watching TV. Prince came bounding in wagging his bottom as he didn't really have a tail (docked short) and then collapsed, I assumed it was one of his turns and went to go and help him up but realised he was dead. It was horrible, Dave and I were stunned but couldn't do anything, mum arrived home and she was very upset. Finally my dad arrived home late that night and tried to bury him in the garden but he was just too big and so sense prevailed in the end and he was taken away. He was a faithful dog and was sadly missed; Timmy the cat had been put to sleep a few years earlier after developing a gangrenous foot and Shandy had long gone to doggie heaven.

Many of my other childhood memories were shared with my best friend, who was a namesake; we would often have sleepovers at each other's houses although we stayed at her house more often than mine as it was a bit bigger. We were friends for many years and her back garden looked out onto our great play area, 'the old tip'. This was an area of waste ground surrounded by back yards of houses in the area. There was an entry into the tip but the house at the side of the entry was lived in by 'Old Man Dick', every kid in the area was frightened of him and he would often chase kids or appear out of nowhere to frighten them. This was a two way hate relationship, kids would shout 'old man Dick' from a distance and he would give chase. Once past Dick's house and onto the tip, we would have great fun.

We built dens on the tip, first made of bricks, then underground, secret dens. Boys would smoke in the dens and you could always hear if anyone was in them as the noise would rise from below ground. Hours and hours were spent playing there. I expect some of the teenagers first romance also occurred in the dens but I was too young at the time to know about this and the older kids would usually clear us off if they wanted to be on their own.

When I was ten, Dawn's brother had his eighteenth birthday party and we were there because it was in their home. I remember drinking quite a few glasses of cider, not knowing what it was, it tasted great and so I had more and more. Eventually I began to feel very peculiar and couldn't speak properly. I thought I was ill. On realising I was drunk; her brother's mates carried me home, put me on my doorstep, knocked the door and scarpered. When my mum answered the door I was sick in the hall, I was sick for ages and felt horrible. On this occasion I think my mum knew a telling off was not necessary, she just looked after me and put me to bed. I have never touched cider from that day to this.

My brother had passed his eleven plus and went to Grammar School but because we lived in a working class area, he was given a hard time for his sins, he also wore NHS glasses and this was a double whammy for him.

'Four eyes! Four eyes!' The local boys would follow him wherever he went, along with, 'snob, snob, toffee nose, grammar school boy.' None of which were true, apart from the latter. Whoever coined the adage 'sticks and stones etc' couldn't have been more wrong, names do hurt children and they can destroy teenagers. I remember him walking along the road one day and getting a dart thrown into his back, his only crime was, he went to Grammar School.

I went to Secondary school where childhood disappears on entering the gates. Fosse Secondary School was a struggling school for working class kids. I admire the ones who managed to become achievers there because they must have been really strong willed, had very supportive families or just been plain gifted. The majority of kids were not there to learn, they had no interest in learning and they were biding their time until leaving. The school leaving age had changed from fifteen and I was going to have to stay on until I was sixteen.

Discipline was a problem, alcohol and drugs were also problems. For the first three years I managed to stay in the top class as it went by ability and so my marks remained constant. By the fourth year, some bright spark decided that the classes should now be divided by alphabetical order of surnames, with no separation of abilities. Chaos was the ensuing result; even if you had wanted to work it was impossible because there were always too many distractions and too much indiscipline. Some teachers managed to keep a bit more discipline than others.

The RE teacher was a nice man who tried to bring kindness into the school but I remember him being attacked by one of the boys during break. The needlework teacher was very supportive of me and I will never forget her kindness at a difficult time. We have kept in touch for years.

In spite of the experience I made some good friends at the school and some of us emerged relatively unscathed. Carla, a black girl, fostered by an elderly white couple stands out as one of my closest friends from the school along with Joni, Maria and Heather. Jackie was also a great friend in my teenage years as she lived nearby although she went to a catholic school and was somewhat better educated.

Joni was a bit of a wildfire, she was always up to something, one night she was babysitting and decided to throw a party, a bad idea, I know. I went to the party and I must say it was already a bit wild when I got there, I remember leaving quite early when I saw that some boys had pulled a door off its hinges. I knew this was not good and went home to bed. In the middle of the night my dad appeared in my bedroom.

'Get downstairs.' He barked. Groggily I got up and went downstairs. My heart sank when I saw Joni and her terrifying dad at the bottom of the stairs. I could see that she had bruises to her face and knew that she had been hit. 'Where were you tonight?' my dad yelled.

'At a party,' I trembled

'Are these yours?' Joni's dad was holding up a pair of knickers. I couldn't believe it.

'No.' I protested, looking horrified.

'Get back to bed.' My dad shouted. I was grounded for a week. Joni's dad had dragged her all around Leicester to everyone's house that had been at the party in the middle of the night with the same routine. I still don't know whose knickers they were but I can confirm they were definitely not mine.

My one and only school trip was to Spain, it was also my first experience of flying and the whole holiday was brilliant. It was a brave group of teachers who took us on holiday but we had a marvellous time. Joni had been told that she couldn't come by her dad after 'Knickergate' but her mum sneaked her out of the house and to the bus leaving from school, we were ecstatic.

I had my first introduction to Bacardi & coke while in Spain and as it was a first trip abroad for most of us. The teachers were relaxed and enjoyed the hotel, the music and the alcohol probably more than we did.

I met my first boyfriend a scrappy fifteen year old with acne, on a Pontin's holiday when I was fourteen, if you can call playing table tennis and a first kiss (peck), a boyfriend. It was a rare family holiday and one that brings back happy memories. On returning from holiday I received a number of letters expressing my new found boyfriend's undying love for me which even at the time I thought was a bit extreme. I have always been a hopeless letter writer and so the relationship, if one can call it that didn't stand the test of time and distance.

My next boyfriend was Pete who was an identical twin – amazingly I could tell the difference and I never liked his brother. Pete was six foot tall, eighteen years old and a bit rough – always in fights, I was sixteen and hated violence. He became obsessed with me and after his initial proposal where he got down on one knee and my refusal he asked me to marry him every time we went out. One night I gave in and said yes but instantly regretted it as he started discussing wedding plans on our way into town. By the end of the conversation I had changed my mind and told him so and shortly after this I ended the relationship. Poor Pete, he was devastated and in a fit of madness he got very drunk and painted my name in five foot high letters on a wall with spray paint and ended up being arrested. I paid the penalty for that later, during my nurse training, when that wall was on my bus route into town and I felt not a little embarrassed for years after until it was finally cleaned off by the council. I never told anyone the huge letters on the wall were there courtesy of me.

There were a few boyfriends after Pete but none serious except for Joe who again treated me with the utmost respect and proposed marriage but was refused on the grounds of I needed to keep my sanity, more on that later in the book.

I finally left school at sixteen, streetwise but with mixed feelings and began my working life, along with all my friends.

Chapter 4

The Nursing Seed Sewn

My childhood ambition was to be a professional tennis player and win Wimbledon. Although I was good at sport and my hand, eye co-ordination was and always has been very good, it was never going to happen. For a start there was no tennis at my school and with no money at home I could only dream. I remember during one summer holiday watching a series on how to play tennis on the television and I would practice hitting a ball at the wall in the back garden for hours.

My first ever job was that of a Comis chef (trainee, come dogsbody) for about nine weeks. I loved the work but the travel and the shifts were hard. The job was in a Wheatsheaf Inn, about fourteen miles and two buses away from where I lived. I had to work two shifts a day, eleven o clock in the morning to three in the afternoon and five until ten in the evening, I can't remember the salary but it was poor. The tips weren't bad though and they were shared out among the staff at the end of a week. I went out with the chef so I could get a lift home at night. I do have a few guilt pangs about that, if you're reading this, although that is highly unlikely, sorry. Poor Dave, he dropped me off outside a disco one Friday night.

'I'll come with you.' He offered.

'Sorry Dave, I'm meeting friends and you would feel left out.' He looked so disappointed. I think he knew I didn't really want to go out with him,

'OK, I'll see you tomorrow.' He started to drive away.

'Yes, I look forward to it, I don't really want to go out tonight but I promised my friends.' I lied, trying to console him and my own guilt pangs. He smiled and waved as I got out of the car. I felt very guilty but this went off all too quickly once inside the disco with my friends.

Of course the relationship with Dave ended when I left the job and I am sure he was much better off without me. During my time at the Wheatsheaf, I learned how to prepare things like prawn cocktail, green salad, and melon starters and cook chicken in the basket, mouth watering stuff. I did like the job and if it were not for the travelling I may have pursued a career in catering ending up as a celebrity chef of course and no, Dave was not hairy biker, Dave.

The next job was working in a handbag warehouse a short distance from my home. I was able to walk to work.

While working at the warehouse, one of my best friends, Maria, whose mother had pre-senile dementia decided to move to Watton in Norfolk. I had never heard of it, Watton that is, not Norfolk, but Maria's sister lived on an RAF base as her brother-in-law was in the navy. I don't know why they lived on an RAF base, probably not enough naval bases and I have to point out, if the naval powers are reading this book, Watton is not by the sea. Her sister was on her own (or soon to be) as her brother in law was embarking on the final sailing of the Ark Royal. This always reminds me of the song by Rod Stewart, 'I Am Sailing' as this last sailing was filmed for a documentary at the time with the song as the soundtrack and we had to watch it ad nauseum.

Maria asked me if I wanted to go to Norfolk with her. I was a bit daunted but I had a sense of adventure and so I didn't hesitate. My mum was obviously sad and I did feel some guilt pangs at leaving her, not sure what my brother felt, he was living his own life between work and the pub. I wouldn't like to say how many times he fell asleep after drinking too much with a cigarette in his hand, waking up to holes in the sheets and mattress. At least he did wake up and didn't manage to set the house on fire, although it wasn't for the want of trying.

After many attempts at giving up smoking myself, particularly after working at the London Chest Hospital and seeing the devastating results of the habit, I finally gave up in 1983 when I was twenty two and like many ex smokers, I now hate the smell of cigarettes.

I started drinking alcohol at around the age of fifteen and used to go to the local pub with schoolmates, starting out with lager and lime. We drank in the same pub as the teachers from our school which was a bit embarrassing at times (probably more so for them). Some disapproved but they didn't give us away. I was never asked my age in spite of looking much younger than I was. I was very sick on a number of occasions though. Occasionally I suffer from vertigo and it brings back memories of nights overloaded with booze. Pernod and black was my tipple for many years until I stopped drinking for around twenty years, not because I was an alcoholic, I might add. I started drinking again after lots of research studies found that red wine helped to prevent heart disease, that's my excuse anyway.

Maria and I moved to RAF Watton which was outside the village, about ten miles from Thetford and twenty miles from Norwich. Maria's sister was ten years older than she was and long before the smoking ban was in place, we had to go outside for a cigarette. We settled in and I think the older sister enjoyed our company for a while. We met one of her friends, Gill who was to become a lifelong friend and who must take full responsibility for me ever becoming a nurse and I will come to that shortly. The first thing we had to do was find a job so that we could pay our way and then find somewhere else to live.

My friend Maria never stepped outside the door without applying make-up; she always had a face full. There was foundation, then eye shadow, mascara and thick black eyeliner. I had never really been one for daytime make-up, for a start I had always loved my bed, being a late nighter, I liked to leave it until the last minute to get up in the mornings. The thought of having to get up at least half an hour earlier to put on make-up was just not me. We needed to find work pretty quickly as Jenny (the older sister) was never going to be a charity, so when we heard that there was some casual labour at an onion farm not too far away and all you had to do was to wait at a certain bus stop at eight o clock in the morning, where a bus picked up workers to take them to the farm, we were there.

'Is this the stop for the onion factory?' I asked a rather rough looking woman who reeked of onions.

'Yes, 'twill be 'ere in a minute' she replied in a Norfolk twang and so we waited until the bus came about five minutes later and by this time there were about twenty women at the stop. We were perhaps a bit cleaner dressed than most of these women seemed to be and when we got on the bus we realised why. The smell of onion hit with force as soon as we stepped inside, everyone had this distinct smell about them. Even the cigarette smoke didn't detract from the smell of onions. Perfume and deodorants are just not designed to permeate through a smell like that, otherwise ours would have helped.

We looked at each other and smiled, after all this was another new adventure. Once we arrived at the farm we followed all the other women and ended up in some open air sheds where we found two spaces next to each other. The idea was to peel as many onions as possible and we would get paid by the tray. We had thought this was going to be easy and a great way to make money quite quickly.

The farm was something like those farmed by

land girls during the war. When the trays arrived there were no large Spanish onions to peel which would fill trays in no time, these were pickled onion size and were going to take forever. It wasn't long before we realised that we were not very good at this, an understatement, I think I had peeled around six onions each when the lady next to me had filled her first tray. This was going to be a very long day and my eyes were already sore and watering, what was worse I was beginning to smell like an onion too. Not long after we started Maria began to panic.

'I can't see, I think I'm going blind,' she cried.

When I looked at her I realised why. Her make-up was all over her face and the more she rubbed the worse it got, eye liner was everywhere as the tears streamed. Tears started to stream down my face but this time not from onions, I was laughing hysterically, it was cruel but I laughed, and laughed and laughed. I don't think any of the other women found it funny, they were so focussed on filling their trays and ignored us totally, probably because they were trying to earn a living and we were just a couple of city kids not taking things seriously enough. I think we had filled half a tray each by lunchtime and we had a very long lunch before joining the bus back to Watton. We didn't even get paid, perhaps it was too difficult to decide how much to pay us. Worse was to come when we arrived back at meticulously house-proud, Jenny's, she wouldn't let us in the house. We had to take our clothes off which went straight into the wash and were sent straight to the bathroom. At least it meant

Jenny didn't mind we were unemployed again.

We had more success with our second job working for Travenol Laboratories in Thetford. The pay was good, even back then, it was thirty eight pounds a week which wasn't a bad salary for seventeen year olds, I earned less when I started nursing. The laboratories made up intravenous fluids that I would later come to use throughout my nursing career. Again, there was a free bus into work and we were taught how to work on each part of the line. We had to wear theatre clothes, not theatrical but hospital operating theatre, white boots, face masks, gloves and net hats to keep everything as sterile as possible. We prepared thousands of bags that were bunged, sealed and then packed. Rotating around the production line prevented it from being too boring but it was pretty boring. The bonus was that as we were now earning a salary, we were able to look for accommodation because I think the novelty of having us was wearing off for Maria's sister.

I had become good friends with Gill who I mentioned earlier and although she was twenty nine and had two children we got on incredibly well. I had not long turned seventeen and felt very grown up. I loved reading and so did Gill from there developed, one of those friendships that survive the tests of time; we always had something to talk about. Facilities on an RAF base are very good and although it is a different world for us civilians I really enjoyed going to the NAFE (shop) and the bars and playing badminton whenever I wanted as I went with

Gill. I used to go to her house and we would chat and drink coffee or wine until around midnight as she also preferred nights to mornings.

Maria and I found a cottage for rent about a mile off the main road to Watton, it was twenty pounds a month and we paid for a month. Shortly after this we had a row. Maria decided to go back to Leicester fairly soon afterwards. I'm sure the row had nothing to do with me of course. Anyway I decided to stay the month out and carry on for that time. I spent some time staying at Gill's as the cottage was a bit isolated and very dark at night, being in the middle of nowhere. I got to know her husband, Craig quite well and the children, Josie and Kevin. The latter two introduced me to the Mr Men by joining me in my bed in the mornings armed with books. I grew to love these books as much as they did.

It was during that month that Gill told me the story about starting her nurse training which she had never completed because she developed a health problem and gave up her training, something she had always regretted. It was clear she had loved nursing and the lightness in her voice as she shared some of her stories was captivating. She was convinced that I should now be a nurse and apply for training.

I am sure that as well as trying to be helpful as she could see that my life was pretty rudderless, she wanted me to fulfil a dream that she had not been able to. It did sound like something I could do and it would beat handbag warehouses and onion farms wouldn't it? She convinced me that it was a

43

good career, as well as being rewarding and as I had no plans in that respect I said I might give it a go although I didn't really know what nursing would be about beyond the fact a nurse worked in a hospital and looked after sick people. I loved the stories Gill would share about the fun she had during her training and the antics she got up to.

I wish I had more philanthropic reasons for beginning my career but I cannot lie. I believe it should be a vocation, a calling, a willingness to sacrifice and do good for the benefit of mankind and that one should have wanted to be a nurse since having a first doll and all that but that wasn't the way I came into it. Thankfully for patients, I don't think I am any less caring as a result. Gill suggested I read a book called One Pair of Feet, by Monica Dickens which I did and found it a hilarious description of nursing in the 1950's but it couldn't be like that now surely? When it came time to say goodbye I think I was ready to return to Leicester but would certainly keep in touch.

I was home again, it was nice to see my mum and Dave and I think we might have had a dad home for a short time. Maria was speaking to me again, thankfully. Unfortunately though, I was unemployed again. This never lasted very long, we are talking days and weeks, not months and years, never long enough to claim benefits.

I completely forgot about nursing for a while and my next job came about through an advert in the local press for an au pair in Belgium. The interview was in Slough near London and I took a train to get there. It was quite exciting now I had the confidence to work away from home. The interview was short and I was asked how to say the children are tired in French and to ask the time. This was fairly elementary, fortunately. I had studied French at school and liked the subject apart from being thrown off the course by a certain teacher who shall remain nameless. I got the job immediately, I must have been the only applicant or perhaps it should have been a warning. A week later I was off to Brussels.

I said goodbye to my poor mum again and my dad took me to London to get the train to Dover where I was to pick up the ferry to Ostend and then a train to Brussels. When I arrived in Brussels I was met by Madam De Ville (the name was chosen deliberately) who was the lady I would be working for, she drove me to Waterloo where the De Ville family lived. I wasn't much on history but could remember that there was a Battle of Waterloo, something to do with Wellington and Napoleon. The De Ville's had three children, Monique, aged seven, Pierre, aged five and a baby of thirteen months called Gerard.

From the moment I entered the house I knew this was not going to be an easy job. My experience of children was zilch, apart from my recent Mr Men readings and babysitting for Maria occasionally, forgot to say she had a baby when she was still at school. I had recently been a child myself of course and these children were going to recreate the Battle of Waterloo, only this time they would win.

My pigeon French was very soon exposed as

they insisted on speaking French to me the whole time (I guess it was their language), which meant I smiled and nodded a lot while not having a clue what was going on. Mme De Ville decided I should attend night school on my evening off in Brussels, I don't recall having any choice in the matter. As I said, the De Ville's spoke to me in French mostly and so I had no idea what was going on half the time. The children spoke no English and it was to be a lonely time until my French picked up. My duties included taking care of the children during the day, as well as housework and cooking (the latter two I had some experience of as my mum had always worked). I had a room in the attic opposite Pierre's which meant there was never any peace. These had to be the children from hell, they never did a thing they were told, Pierre was forever playing with matches and Mme De Ville spoilt them rotten (probably because she didn't have to spend any time with them) and was no-where near firm enough with Pierre who was a monster. Wednesday evenings were spent taking a tram which was the highlight of my week, into Brussels for my evening class where the teacher also took the class in French and I often left no wiser than when I entered.

One evening I was informed I would be babysitting by Mme De Ville as she and her husband were going to play Bridge in Paris. I know, popping out from Waterloo for a game of Bridge in Paris, this was a different world to the one I came from. On this particular evening I had finally got the children to go to bed which was a feat in itself and was sitting downstairs watching television which I didn't understand. Suddenly the lights went out and the TV went off. Pierre came running into the room shouting excitedly and as he was naturally scared of the dark, he tremblingly took me by the hand, to show me where the electricity meter was and I was trying to calm him down, explaining that we would soon have the lights on again.

When we got to the second staircase leading to the attic rooms I was horrified to see flames pouring out of his bedroom, I could smell acrid smoke, the fire had really taken hold, and I began to feel very hot, not sure whether this was panic or heat from the fire. There was no fire extinguisher to hand, not that I even thought to look for one as this was a real FIRE and could not be tackled by a seventeen year old amateur. I managed to wake Monique, who slept on the first floor and had the foresight grab the baby from his cot, a miracle on reflection and then ran downstairs with crying children and a baby tucked under my arm.

I had no idea how to phone the fire brigade and so telephoned the lady across the road whose name was on a pad by the phone and managed to shout,

'FEU, FEU.' Thank you French teacher. Fortunately the lady understood and called the fire brigade who were there within minutes. In the meantime I had taken the children out of the house and into the street. It was a cold, dark night as I recall and the flames were clearly visible from the road. The neighbour called the De Ville's back from their Bridge evening. Chaos reigned for a few hours and I remember when I finally got to my room that night it was damp where the firemen had been through to get to Pierre's room with hoses and the walls were black, the smell was that of burnt wood but I had to sleep in it nevertheless. The next morning Mme De Ville managed to sheepishly thank me for saving the children's lives. Pierre was given a very mild scolding about playing with matches that, in my opinion could have been a little more forceful as I would have happily strangled him.

The day after the fire, I decided that I would leave at the earliest opportunity and this was soon to come by way of a letter from home. My mum wrote to say that my dad hadn't returned home after dropping me off in London. This was no surprise to me because this was often the case. I did, however, seize the opportunity to show Mme De Ville the letter and explain that I needed to return home to search for a missing parent. Mme De Ville thought that my mother was colluding with me to give me an excuse to leave as she said she had had many au pairs who made up all sorts of stories in order to leave, how surprising, I thought.

A few weeks later, Mme De Ville reluctantly took me to Brussels station on the Saturday but still refused to pay me, she said she would pay me when I came back, as if that was likely, in your dreams, I thought. This was the second job I had in my life where I received no pay.

Once home and unemployed again, I met an old school friend called Jan at the bus stop a week or so later and discovered she was working in a supermarket, she offered to ask the manager if there were any jobs for me. About a week later I started working at Belco Supermarket in Leicester. Twice a week the Belco bus, which was literally a double decker bus turned into a mobile supermarket, went out to different areas of Leicester to sell goods to the more out of the way areas. I usually did one of these days and loved it. The bus was driven by a senior manager and he always took me to lunch at the Post House Hotel (not just me, whoever was working the till on the bus days) and for someone who had never been in a hotel this was a real treat.

It was during my time working at Belco that I finally got around to applying for nurse training (probably due to nagging from Gill), I also applied to join the WRENS. I didn't get into the WRENS because I kept showing protein in my urine, no idea why and it didn't appear again. In retrospect I'm pleased I wasn't accepted as I don't think I would have liked the discipline, nursing was bad enough but nursing and the WRENS, I think that might have been regimental overload.

When I told my mum I was going to apply for nurse training she wasn't as supportive as I thought she would be and asked if I was sure I could do it and that I might not pass the exams. I think it was more likely to be because she had seen her father die of bowel cancer aged just thirty six, she would have been twelve years old then and not many years later she gave up work to nurse her mother who died of ovarian cancer at the age of fifty. I am sure she was trying to protect me from the trauma that she had been through as a child and an older sister. My mother was not a person who opened up her feelings but she was very frightened of the word cancer.

I left Belco Supermarket with mixed feelings as I had enjoyed the work there but I knew I had finally made the right decision regarding nursing.

As mentioned previously, the first few months of training took place at Charles Frears School of Nursing in Leicester, yet again two buses away, where we had our initial classroom study. The school was to become a regular feature throughout the two years of training as we had our ward placements followed by two weeks in the school learning our theory. In my second year I ended up renting a bedsit across the road from the school of nursing and then, you guessed it, there were two buses to get to the hospital.

My first month's salary was around eighty pounds. I needed bank loans on a rolling basis. Not so different to anyone about to embark on a university education now. It took most of us ten to fifteen years to get out of debt because the pay was so low even after qualifying, does this sound familiar?

I often asked myself what I was doing sitting in a classroom of forty six girls (not one male in my training set), learning anatomy and physiology. Mrs Butcher took us through all of the bodily systems, for which I am now very grateful because we learnt such a lot, but I wasn't used to studying and found it very difficult to get into it.

During training we covered the basic anatomy and physiology of the respiratory, cardiovascular, nervous, genito-urinary and musculo-skeletal systems, as well as the skin. Basic observations included temperature, pulse and blood-pressures were mastered, then bed baths, shaves, pressure area checks, turns, lifts, wound dressings, mouth cleaning, rectal examination, enemas, catheterisation (female only initially), catheter changes, insertion and removal of naso-gastric tubes, fitting, and emptying colostomy bags, the list is endless. Everything was taught very thoroughly and it was all a lot more complicated than it sounds even giving a bed bath. There was a life sized skeleton in the corner of the practice room and we would spend hours trying to name all the bones.

I have not performed a bed bath for many years as these are done by heath care assistants in hospitals and social services home carers in patients homes but I can still remember this and many other procedures which I learned by rote. I am not so sure that talcum powder was such a good idea though, we would shake it liberally, all over patients, especially the intimate areas, but they did smell nice. I'm surprised there aren't more nurses with respiratory diseases after breathing in all that talc filled air. Obviously learning in the classroom is one thing and doing these things to real live patients is another. After two months of the classroom it was time to be let loose on the wards.

Chapter 5

Bedpans and Walking Sticks

Looking back on it, I was really fortunate with my first ward, I think it was this ward that made me fall in love with nursing and never look back. I was very happy to be assigned to male orthopaedics it was going to be good. I loved it from the moment I started. One thing I learned very quickly was that if the sister was a good one, the ward ran like clockwork and it tended to be a happy place to work, no matter how busy it was. This was going to be one of those wards, the sister was always in the background keeping things ticking over and she had a superb Staff Nurse who was a really good trainer. I learned so much even though I was not supernumerary like students are today and I had no specified mentor, the term only applied to the martial arts back in 1977, not to nursing.

Everything I learned was through hands on care or observation, senior students often took on the role of teacher/trainer and I was frequently working with a third year student nurse called Alex, female version, short for Alexandra. Alex was a pretty freckle faced girl with red hair, she was one of the first people I met on working there and we hit it off straight away although we came from very different backgrounds. Her family were middle class professionals, her father being a lawyer and her mother a teacher, she cooked me my first ever spaghetti bolognaise that didn't come out of a tin and I never looked back.

'Do you want to come to our flat after work I'm cooking spaghetti?' Alex had asked, a simple question, I pictured the tin of Heinz Spaghetti.

'That would be great.' I had replied. I went back to her flat straight from work as it would have been too far to go home first on the two buses. The flats were nice, the nursing home for third years was a high rise block, not far from the hospital and mostly there were four people sharing. The building was not old like the hospital. I liked it, it was relatively tidy. Alex's flatmates were all at work on late shifts or out. We were having a great chat in the kitchen and she started to prepare dinner.

I had never seen real spaghetti or mince, having been brought up on tinned and processed foods I must have been really unhealthy. To this day I remember faggots that formed a weekly part of my childhood diet, tinned spaghetti and tinned meat pies. I tried not to give myself away, it's not as if I had never cooked, I had been cooking meals since I was twelve years old but the only fresh parts were the potatoes and veggies. Although fresh may not have been the best term as the veggies were almost always nearing rotten, if they had had a best before date, it would have been long past. I probably had given myself away when I looked at the bolognaise sauce remnants on my uniform when I got home! Alex was very polite and didn't appear to notice when I was trying to work out how to get the spaghetti in my mouth without slurping or at least she gave that impression. I had a lot of learning to do and it obviously didn't confine itself to the wards.

The Leicester Royal Infirmary was a large old hospital and the ward was referred to as a Nightingale ward. The entrance was via two sets of double doors, once through the first set there was a medical room with stainless steel trolleys and cupboards containing dressings and equipment, also IV fluids were kept in there in boxes, there was a side room and a kitchen, after this, through the next set of doors was the main ward. A long ward with marble floors and twenty beds down each side, patients faced each other and shouted across the ward to converse and banter, especially on male orthopaedics. The ceiling was mega high and the windows reminded me of those found in churches but without the stained glass.

A long table ran down the centre and this is where we would sit and write up the Kardex. Each patient's nursing records were kept in a Kardex card filing system inside a large metal type clipboard about six inches wide, which opened like a stack of cards in alphabetical order. It was called the Kardex which was a brand name of the company that made it. At the end of a shift the Kardex for each patient was completed by the nurse looking after that patient, this often meant filling in fifteen to twenty records per shift. A lot of repetitive information was written in the Kardex, such as:

- Slept well

- No complaints
- Comfortable
- Sat out

We were not allowed to sit at the nurses' station, a semi circular desk area on the left as you entered the ward where only Sister and Staff Nurses sat – in fact we were rarely allowed to sit at all. The patients' medical notes were kept in a filing trolley on wheels by the nurses' station and also the medicines trolley was in that area. At the end of the ward, on the far left was the sluice area where bedpans were washed, an area to which I would become intimately acquainted; other equipment such as commodes, enema equipment, urine testing equipment and glass urinals were also kept there.

The bedpans were stainless steel and I spent many hours of my twelve week placement in the sluice, emptying bedpans and then putting them into the a huge machine called an Autoclave. I wish I'd kept count because with the majority of the men in traction they all needed daily bedpans and having ones bowels opened regularly was a must otherwise something would need to be given to force the issue. In fact, one of the first things I learned was to ask a patient every day if they had had their bowels opened. Initially I found this a bit embarrassing; after all there were a lot of boys my age on this ward. Cleaning the bedpans that didn't come out of the washer totally clean and shiny was also part of the probationer role and that was just disgusting.

The bedpans were really cold to sit on

(according to patients) unless a kind nurse ran them under hot water first which depended on what side of bed the nurse had got out of that day. The urinals were made of glass and these too were emptied and washed in the Autoclave but with extreme care. All the commodes had to be washed down and disinfected daily and of course that too was one of my jobs. There were cleaners of course and they kept the floors, bathrooms and surfaces absolutely pristine in spite of the age of the building. It was a nurse's job though to wash down mattresses, pillows that were encased in plastic and patient lockers on discharge. They were disinfected and every part of the bed was washed down including all the metal parts.

Cleaners kept the area under beds spotless and lockers were moved out daily to clean underneath. The buffers that polished floors came out every evening and were part of the daily ward ritual, while nurses on the late shift gave out hot drinks to patients. During my first week I was to do the evening drinks rounds where milky drinks were made, I used to dread a patient saying they wanted horlicks, it was impossible to make. The first time I made it I thought it was just like ovaltine, so I put a couple of spoons of horlicks in a glass of hot milk and stirred. I was left with lumps of horlicks floating on top of the milk and the patient looked horrified. One of the Nursing Auxiliary's saw my mistake and took over.

'You have to mix it with a bit of cold milk first in a cup or jug and once it's in a paste you gradually stir in the milk, as if you were making Béchamel Sauce.' She explained. Béchamel sauce? What the heck was that? Anyway I soon learned the technique although I don't think I was ever brilliant at it, just good enough to get through the drinks rounds. I was certainly beginning to feel a sense of inadequacy, I hadn't imagined that nursing would include teaching me how to make hot milky drinks. I thought that was something I already knew but obviously not.

Another one of my first jobs was to help dish out meals at meal times. A huge, heated metal trolley would be brought onto the ward at roughly the same time every day. The porters would bring the trolley up from the kitchen. Half an hour before the meal trolley was due we would make sure the bed tables were put in place over the beds so that the men in bed could get at their meals. Once the meal trolley arrived it was all hands on deck, at least, all student hands on deck. The meals came plated up and were hot, sometimes the plates were too hot if the trolley arrived very quickly from the main kitchens. Each meal had a card on top with the patient's name and so it was relatively easy to dish the meals out except when the patient would change his mind and want something else. This was not unusual as they would choose their meals after breakfast and by the time evening came they wanted something different. Whilst we tried to accommodate, it was not always possible if there were not enough spare meals. Extras were always added to the trolley for any new patients who may have been admitted during the day.

Once the meals were distributed, we would help anyone who needed assistance with feeding or cutting up the food. It was difficult sometimes to go at the patient's pace as we were always so busy and some patients did find the constant shovelling of a fork into their mouths a bit trying. It was hard not to assist with feeding on autopilot and be thinking of the next thing on the list that I had to do, especially when I was new and this was when I had to be more careful not to choke the poor person I was trying to help. Thankfully, I didn't manage to choke anyone, at least not with food, it was much harder with drinks as the temptation to give too much too fast was ever present.

One time a patient I was helping with a drink, started to cough and splutter and I was scared into submission and then I really did slow down, it was terrifying. There was no way I wanted Mrs Butcher to ask me to leave through carelessness.

The toilets at the end of the ward were really cold, the windows were kept open to reduce odours and the wind from these would gust right through the ward sometimes sending papers flying. There were two enormous cast iron baths in the toilet area separated by a wall rather than by doors. They were very much in demand for those not in plaster or traction.

There was a huge toilet chair that patients were sat on and then wheeled to the bath and lowered in while still sitting on this. The first time I bathed a man using this contraption was an experience in itself. It took two to manage the unwieldy beast as it was cumbersome and not the safest mode of transport.

'I'm just going to lower you into the bath now Mr Blake,' I tried to sound confident. Mr Blake was suspended in mid air over the bath, holding on to the side handles for dear life, while he was lowered into the bath with me letting him down gradually while turning a handle on a wheel that controlled the mechanism. A third year student called Flo was helping Mr Blake to stay seated and not slide off during this manoeuvre.

'I've got your legs, Mr Blake, you try and stay still,' at this point he had started to wriggle a bit, probably because I had been a bit over enthusiastic with the lowering mechanism. 'Slow down a bit,' instructed Flo. Finally Mr Blake had landed at the bottom of the bath and we could all breathe a sigh of relief, particularly me. The easy part was the bathing as long as the patient didn't try to drown themselves by throwing themselves around which sometimes happened, thankfully this didn't happen with Mr Blake and my first handling of the patient and equipment had gone relatively smoothly. The difficult part was yet to come as I realised that turning the wheel to raise the seat was a bit more arduous. Nevertheless with a little encouragement from both Mr Blake and Flo, I managed to successfully return him to safety.

In between the sluice and the toilets, at the end of the ward there was a day room with comfy chairs and a television. Smoking was allowed in hospital day rooms and the patients who weren't attached to traction would congregate to smoke and watch TV. TV consisted of just three channels; BBC1, BBC2 & ATV (became Central Independence TV in 1982). The day room was always very foggy and unhealthy compared to today's standards where smoking is not allowed in any part of a hospital. Leading off the right hand side of the ward was an enclosed balcony that had glass windows and doors leading outside, with about six beds for recuperating patients who could look out onto a little bit of greenery.

Male orthopaedics had a larger proportion of young men than most wards as it tended to be young men who broke their bones mostly from motorbike and car accidents. It should have made us more aware of the dangers of driving and should definitely put anyone but the insane off motorbikes. Many motorcyclists never made it to the ward as they died at the site of the accident or on the way to hospital. Some still didn't wear crash helmets, in spite of it being made compulsory to wear them in 1973. Of course it didn't put me off then because like most eighteen year olds, I knew that these things only happened to other people and that I was immortal. I did in fact ride a Suzuki 125 for a few years in my early twenties during my RGN training and came off it on more than one occasion but thankfully got away with cuts and bruises.

I went out with a guy called Mike for a while and rode pillion on his BMW motorbike which I always found exhilarating. It was less exhilarating when, after going out with him for several months he proposed to me, at the same time confessing he was married. I had a general principal not to go out with a married man and I was furious with myself for not suspecting that the reason we went out so rarely and always went to pubs in the countryside was not because of his love of nature but because he was married. I was furious with him for misleading me, the marriage proposal obviously didn't go the way he intended as I told him to get lost (might have been a bit stronger language) and indignantly walked away, thankfully I never saw him again.

I found out personally on two occasions that motorbikes offered little protection in a crash. The first did not involve me directly but a friend. When he was nineteen he got a job out in the countryside somewhere and was riding home one night on his motorbike, he took a bend too quickly and was thrown off, unfortunately his back was slammed against a tree causing it to break. He was admitted to a hospital that specialised in back injuries but his spine was broken and he was declared paraplegic meaning that he was numb from the waist down. This was a high price to pay for one mistake but it demonstrates just how vulnerable a person is when on these fast machines. The human body is strong but cannot withstand that sort of impact. He took it badly and although initially he appeared to be coping positively with the wheelchair confined life, he started to take unnecessary risks almost as if he had a death wish and I met him a few years later. He had long since left home and was living in a flat where he was self neglecting so much that he had developed pressure sores and his flat was in a mess. He was obviously embarrassed to see me like this and I was deeply saddened, I did my best to try to encourage him and in addition to dressing his wounds I cleaned up his flat and tried to motivate him to get his life back.

'I don't have a life.' He said, 'girls aren't interested, they just feel sorry for me and I can't feel anything, there is nothing out there for me.' I remembered he had been in a wheelchair basketball team when he had first come out of hospital,

'What about the basketball team?' I suggested.

'I can't play because I keep getting these pressure sores,' he retorted. We spoke for a while but I realised that he was depressed and needed more support, I suggested he speak to his GP and try to get help. I was very sad when I left because I knew nothing was going in. His mum was very supportive and visited regularly but even she wasn't able to motivate him during this time, I like to think that he has since turned the corner and got his life back together in a more positive way.

Some of the district nurses regularly looking after him were a bit fed up with him but it is so important to remember that things are not always the way they seem. I had known him in a different life but they hadn't, they just saw an awkward young man self neglecting while they had other patients with terminal cancer to look after and so the empathy swingometer wasn't going in his favour.

The next event was a little closer to home. In my early thirties while on holiday in Switzerland I was to come into close contact with a motorbike again, too close by far. I was visiting a friend called Marie-Claude and her parents met me at the airport. They decided to show me a little bit of Geneva before we drove to Lausanne where they lived. I was following them across the road when Marie-Claude's mum suddenly looked back and cried out, I turned to look where she was looking and instantly saw a motorcycle heading directly for me. There was no time to react, it hit me in the ribs and I ended up floored in the middle of the road with a fractured wrist and foot, I realised how lucky I was to be alive and thanked God it was not a car. The ironic thing about it all was that if Marie-Claude's mum had not cried out I would have continued across the road and the bike would have missed me but it was one of those instants where everything happens so quickly and life and the realisation of human frailty flash before you and then it is over. You either survive or you don't.

When the ambulance took me to hospital it reminded me of orthopaedics. I was very efficiently plastered up and discharged which was fortunate because I didn't have any holiday insurance. It cost me five hundred pounds for the X Rays and the privilege. I was grateful to the English radiographer who, after realising I was not insured, kindly lost the chest X rays once she had checked I did not have a punctured lung. The rest of the holiday, if it could be called that was spent trying to adjust to walking on a broken foot without crutches as I couldn't hold them due to my broken wrist being on the same side.

We managed to make the best of my visit and Marie-Claude was a great hostess. I was glad I decided to continue the holiday as it turned out that it was the last time I would see my very dear friend. A year later Marie-Claude developed a brain tumour and died just a few weeks afterwards, I didn't even hear about this until after the funeral which was devastating, she was one of the nicest people I had known.

About three months after the holiday the Swiss added insult to injury by sending me a fine demanding the equivalent of sixty pounds for crossing the road in the wrong place. This was also the first time in my life I had three weeks in a row off sick – I was a midwife at the time. I had been signed off for six weeks but I healed quickly and then pleaded with my GP to let me go back to work – I was not used to sitting around at home.

Back to male orthopaedics, on my first day I got to do an observations round down one side of the ward. These rounds were done four hourly on every ward without fail throughout my training and beyond.

'Temperature, pulse and respirations, TPR for short, along with blood pressure measurements are very important nurses.' Explained Mrs Butcher during our first week of training, 'these measurements will alert you to signs of infection, hypothermia, respiratory and cardiac conditions as well as shock, thrombosis and many other conditions so don't ever underestimate their value.' I think I must have drifted off during the rest of the lecture but I do remember thinking hypothermia was stretching it as you only got that in freezing cold conditions (little did I know). We had practised on each other during the training sessions and it was an area I felt competent in.

The mercury containing thermometers which are no longer used due to the dangers of mercury spills, (I should be dead now because I witnessed many spills during my career) were kept above the patient's bed in a container with some pink coloured disinfectant in the bottom. We would use a trolley to do the TPR round with everything we needed on top, mercury containing blood pressure machines and sterile wipes to wipe the thermometer before and after putting it in the patient's mouth. The hardest part of this procedure was shaking the thermometer to get the mercury down below thirty six degrees centigrade (my training started shortly after the move from using Fahrenheit as the temperature measurement although I was brought up using the latter). Some of the thermometers took a lot of wrist flicking and until the art was mastered my rounds took twice as long as the more experienced students. My round got complicated when I got to Mr Graham.

'Good morning Mr Graham, I am just going to take your temperature.' No response, Mr Graham was staring at the ceiling. I tried speaking a bit louder, trying to sound more confident than I felt.

'Don't worry nurse, he doesn't speak.' Said the

man next to him,

'Oh.' I said not feeling very sure what that meant or what to do next. Staff nurse Brody was about to pass, 'Staff' I called, 'I am doing the round and not sure how to take Mr Graham's temperature.' Staff Brody took the thermometer from my hand,

'Mr Graham,' she said gently, 'I am just going to take your temperature' and as she offered the thermometer to his mouth, he opened it and held it perfectly under his tongue. 'It's okay nurse, you'll get the hang of this.' She smiled and walked on. I managed to complete the procedure also taking his pulse which had to be counted for a full minute and his respiratory rate. I had been taught that the latter had to be taken while holding the pulse so as not to alert the patient to the fact that you were counting the respirations otherwise they might breathe differently. Mr Graham's blood pressure was taken in much the same way as the temperature, I explained what I was going to do and he offered his arm for the cuff to be wrapped around. Mr Graham, I later found out had suffered a head injury and although he was able to understand everything that was said to him, he had been left mute and did not engage with those around him.

Many men on the orthopaedic ward were in traction with the leg placed in a metal brace and weights holding the broken leg in place. These were suspended at the end of the bed and of course the rookie nurse at some stage would bump into or dislodge the weights causing the patient to shout some obscenity, some would laugh hysterically because they knew that you were new to the game, others were not so forgiving.

Boyish pranks were common and they always took pleasure in winding up the new girls. If it wasn't the constant, 'Hurry up nurse, I need a bedpan.' It was 'Nurse, hurry up, I need a bottle (urinal).' I was once pulled onto the lap of one of the boys in a wheelchair who then raced up and down the ward doing wheelies and skid turns, fortunately Sister was not on the ward at the time. Bed bathing young men was initially embarrassing but the boys were just as embarrassed as I was except for exhibitionists who would try to get a young nurse to help them with the urinal.

'It's your leg that's broken not your hands.' I would smile sweetly. I had learned how to handle this situation very soon after starting on the ward. The ward was always full and always busy so, as well as the fun there was a lot of hard work and a few personalities that stand out.

Shift work was not entirely new to me as I had worked for a year at the supermarket in Leicester and would work one late shift a week and most Saturdays. Hospital shifts were entirely different though; your body never knew what was coming next. One day I was starting at the crack of dawn and the next day at lunchtime which wasn't so bad but sometimes we had to work what was commonly known as the 'ten day stretch,' consisting of lates and earlies over ten days. The late, early shifts were the killer; I would finish work at half past nine in the evening, probably go to the pub after work with a few other nurses and then get up at six o clock in the morning, the next day to be in for the early shift.

The shift patterns initially were quarter past seven in the morning to a quarter past five in the afternoon (earlies) and half past twelve to half past nine (lates) with one half hour break on the early and two fifteen minute breaks and two half hour breaks on the late. On top of that we were on our feet all day long, I must have walked miles in a day and my legs ached at the end of the shift, if we had worn pedometers I would estimate a student nurse walked at least five miles every day.

Nurses feet are an occupational hazard, nylon tights in tight leather shoes, walking for miles; smelly, sweaty feet were the end result and as for the smell of the shoes! Amazingly, the body adjusted to shifts, which was a miracle because I just hated early morning wakening. At one point during my career I used to put the alarm clock in a saucepan at the opposite side of the room so that I would have to get out of bed to switch it off. The theory being that I would then get up but I can tell you that some days I walked over to the alarm half asleep, switched it off and went back to bed and to sleep. Night shifts came a bit later in the training.

There are some routines that stand out which are now a part of nursing history and every nurse over a certain age can remember. Every bed was on wheels and all of the wheels had to face in the same direction, inwards. I don't ever remember anyone telling me to do this although I would think someone did. When you looked down the ward all of the wheels would be perfectly aligned, I have no idea how this helped people get better but in these days of Feng Shui there may be a perfectly logical reason. I admit to giving a wheel an occasional kick to put it out of line much to the annoyance of the Nursing Officer (matrons had recently disappeared in favour of the more modern nursing officer), who would arrive to carry out spot checks. Hospitals have since gone back to matrons again although not quite the same as the matrons from the 1960s.

We did pressure care rounds, commonly known as 'bum' rounds every two to four hours depending on the dependency of the patient, many on the orthopaedic ward (young and old) were confined to bed. These rounds included washing and vigorously rubbing the patient's buttocks with soap and water in order to get the circulation going and prevent pressure sores. It wasn't just bums of course, we did elbows and heels as well and it was the pressure relieving and position changing rather than the rubbing that prevented the sores. The young lads were taught to lift themselves up every hour using the 'Monkey Poles' above their heads. Pressure sores were seen as poor nursing and woe betide any ward that allowed sores to develop, sometimes patients were admitted with sores and occasionally due to friction from sliding up and down the beds themselves or through ill health, small ones would occur. Some nurses were a little more vigorous than others in the pursuit of bum rubbing and may have unwittingly done more harm than good. I won't comment on whether some may have enjoyed it more than they should or were just plain sadistic.

All sorts of things were applied to bums after the washing and these included talcum powder, spirit, creams or oil depending on where you trained. If a patient dared to develop a pressure sore one of the treatments for this was egg white and oxygen. The patient would be turned onto their side and the offending area exposed, egg white was applied to the wound using a pastry brush, no I'm kidding it was applied with a sterile gauze swab, a piece of oxygen tubing was then taped to the patient's bottom to keep it in place and then the oxygen was turned on fairly high. The theory being that the protein from the egg white would work with the oxygen supplied directly to the wound to promote wound healing. I am amazed that nobody ever went up in smoke considering how close the day rooms with the smokers' in were to the wards with all this oxygen flowing.

We also did regular 'bottle' rounds and on male orthopaedics it wasn't always urine found in the bottles, sometimes the boys would put raspberry drinks in them to try to get us to think it was blood. Sometimes there was blood of course and we had to measure it and record on an input and output chart, inspect the urine for colour and test it once a day. Testing urine for glucose was done in test tubes back then, where a few drops of urine were placed in a tube, along with a tablet that turned to the appropriate colour if glucose was present, this is much simpler now with urine dipsticks that can test for almost everything. A different tablet and test tube was used to test for ketones and litmus strips were used to test the Ph of urine.

Dressing rounds were always done in the afternoon after all the bed making, washing and cleaning had finished, when the dust had settled as it were. All wounds were dressed and these were done in twos, there was always a 'clean' nurse who dressed the wounds and a 'dirty' nurse who opened all the sterile packs for the clean nurse. This was in no way a comment on either of the nurses' personal hygiene or moral habits. Every nurse has her favourite activity and for some reason I loved removing stitches. I was in my element when as a midwife I learnt to stitch and would take great pride in my handiwork when stitching women's perineum's after childbirth,

The dressing regimes were taken very seriously as the last thing that anyone wanted was for the patient to end up with an infection Particular care was taken to clean around the pins (more like huge nails) that went through the patients' legs into the bones as bone infections were very difficult to treat. There were myriads of wounds that I came across on this first ward experience as people following falls, car and motorcycle accidents didn't just break bones they were often left with other injuries too. Dressing rounds were probably my favourite chores and I always enjoyed being the clean nurse once I had developed the skill. We used metal forceps to hold everything such as sterile cotton wool, gauze and dressings and this took an element of dexterity.

Later in my training one of the Clinical Tutors would assess my dressing technique as we had a number of Practical assessments to pass as well as final exams. The forceps would all be sent to a different part of the hospital after use for re-sterilisation.

The orthopaedic consultant and his entourage would do a daily ward round and patients were not allowed to use a commode or be wheeled to the toilet while this was taking place. Any noise was treated with a 'tut, tut' by the consultant and woe betide any patient who dared ring his buzzer. Sister always had to be on duty or at least a Senior Staff Nurse and quiet had to be maintained for the duration and the Student Nurses had to go to the sluice out of the way.

Many surgeons were and still can be quite pompous but I have also met some who are quite normal and yes, surgeons do sometimes have affairs with theatre sisters and/or scrub nurses. It must be those long hours gazing into each other's eyes over an unconscious patient. I have never known a female surgeon have an affair with a nurse as there weren't many of them about when I started out but I'm sure it happens. Nurses and doctors do sometimes go out with each other and some marry although this doesn't happen at the frequency that Casualty or Holby City would have us believe.

The nurses' uniform is a long standing tradition which stems back, I think to dear Florence Nightingale. Little did she know that the nurse uniform would become a slushy stereotypical object of desire, the 'Carry On' films have a lot to answer for.

My first uniform was plain white cotton, polyester mix which was see-through, totally impractical in terms of colour and design. The uniforms had arrived during our PTS and we had been so excited to receive them, we had three dresses, a navy Macintosh which was our outdoor uniform and a navy cape for walking around the hospital grounds and cardboard hats. We absolutely loved the capes but as there were no real grounds to wander in at the Leicester Royal I would have to wait until I was based at Groby Road to wear mine. The live in girls got to wear theirs to cross the road from the nursing home to the hospital. As I travelled in by bus it was the Macintosh that I would wear mostly.

Uniforms were laundered in house through the laundry which could be quite tricky when we only had three and worked full time and I lost a beautiful silver cross my cousin had bought me when it was sent to the laundry unwittingly in my uniform pocket and never returned. Whilst the uniform may have been nice for the patients, it used to ride up as soon as you bent down to do anything, it needed a full length under slip which I had never worn prior to nurse training (made me feel like a granny) and the colour was totally inappropriate when dealing with blood, gore, vomit and all the other bodily fluids that nurses came into contact with. Nevertheless I was so proud to put it on and when I walked on to my first ward wearing it, I felt I had arrived. I did love all the pockets and felt very proud to put my scissors and pens in one of the breast pockets and with my fob watch pinned onto the uniform.

We didn't get belts in the first year of training but were given them during second and third years. During my enrolled nurse training the belt was green and then navy during my RGN training.

We wore hats that were equally impractical and made of cardboard with various stripes depicting the type and year of training. First year students had one stripe on their hat, blue for SRN trainee and green for SEN, second years' two stripes and third years' three. There was an art to making up the hats and then attaching them to the hair with grips but it was soon to be mastered, although I think my hat would occasionally hang at half mast although, amazingly it didn't get knocked off very often in spite of all the lifting and lugging of patients that we did. Sisters and staff nurse got to wear proper starched frilly material hats and the staff nurses' hat was lovely with pleats at the back.

Prior to training we were sent a list of items to buy (out of our own money). These included a fob watch which I kept for years, pocket pen and torch holders, a pen-torch; blunt end nurses scissors and black leather lace up shoes. We were not allowed to wear make-up, had to keep our finger nails short, no nail varnish, no jewellery (except wedding ring or stud ear rings, nose studs were not in fashion back then) and no wrist watch. Much of this has recently been re-introduced into nursing as part of the drive to reduce hospital acquired infection; along with hand washing as it had become apparent that some millennium nurses had forgotten how to wash their hands. Doctors, I have to say have never been renowned for washing their hands, with the exception of surgeons who would be supervised by a theatre sister.

Many doctors seemed to feel that bacteria only attached themselves to nurses and that once they got their medical degree the bacteria went around them and onto everyone else.

The nurses' buckle was a part of the uniform we were so proud of, as this could only be worn after qualifying and it was often bought by proud parents and then sewn onto the belt with love and worn with pride. My mum bought me a silver buckle which certainly fitted that category when I qualified and I still have it tucked away, although it is not worn these days, mainly because the belt wouldn't fit around my expanded waist but also because they are no longer required as nurses' uniforms have changed with many now wearing trousers and tunics.

One of the first patients' who stands out to me was Sam or should I say Sam and his father. Sam was twenty seven and had suffered a head injury from a car accident and like many in the late 1970's he had been driving without a seatbelt and thrown through the windscreen. Seatbelts were made mandatory for drivers and passengers in 1983. He was in the first bed after the Nurses' Station; patients who were the most ill were kept close to the Nurses' Station and moved down the ward according to recovery. Dying patients were always in beds near the beginning of the ward. Sam was semi-conscious for my first few weeks on the ward and fed via intravenous infusion. He needed help with everything at first. His father, John visited every day and we would chat while I was caring for Sam.

Sam had no idea where he was or who he was, he had stitches to his head where the surgeon had operated to relieve bleeding pressure from the brain and his head had been shaved, he had spiky bits of black hair coming through when I started on the ward and he was beginning to speak, albeit a bit like a child learning to say their first words. Fortunately the ward Sister did allow you to chat to patients and relatives, unlike some ward Sisters who would tell you off for wasting time talking, even to patients. John was a divorcee in his forties, it wasn't long before he was asking me out. In fact when Sam got better they both asked me out which could have been very complicated. I refused the date offer but did become friends with John and found out he was a DJ. He asked if I fancied doing the occasional session as he had musical equipment for parties and clubs but he didn't like the talking bit. At first I thought he was joking but he asked me if I fancied giving it a go and I was always keen for a new adventure, particularly as women DJs were almost unheard of back then. I thought it couldn't be that hard and I had the gift of the gab so worth a shot especially as I would be paid too?

The one and only time I did this we went to a club somewhere out in the country – fortunately it wasn't a ploy to get me on a date. We arrived at the club and went backstage and I waited while John set up the equipment. I went on stage and sat behind the microphone rattling away, playing some really good records from the 60's and 70's, wondering why no-one was dancing. I didn't feel it was going that well and there was a peculiar atmosphere but I carried on regardless. It was quite dark and there was a lot of noise, once my eyes became accustomed to the darkness I could see that the room was full of men, not a woman to be seen. Once my time was up I went backstage and met a woman who was about to go on. I explained that the audience was a bit dreary and not very likely to respond and then naively I asked her what she did, she casually said she was a stripper and finally the penny dropped. No wonder they didn't dance. John swore to me, he didn't know it was a strip club and there began and ended my career as a DJ.

Sam gradually got better but still couldn't remember much about his former life, in fact, the really sad thing was that he couldn't remember he had an estranged wife and it was very hard for her. She did visit occasionally but he really couldn't remember who she was and as they were separated anyway she must have felt it was not worth the emotional strain on either of them and stopped visiting. Sam did eventually go home and we kept in touch for a while and his father and I remained friends for about a year or so, he even drove me to the airport when I was flying to Malta to visit Gill and Craig as they had moved from Watton and Craig was now stationed in Malta, my gain. The

RAF left Malta in 1979 so I was lucky to go when I did in 1978 as Gill wanted an update on my training.

I flew out to Malta on my own (this was only my second time flying) and landed at RAF Luqa which also served as a civilian airport. The airport was near to the capital city of Valetta and we managed a few shopping trips there. Gill and Craig met me at the airport along with Josie and Kevin who were now aged seven and five. Gill couldn't wait to be filled in on hospital gossip and we quickly caught up where we had left off two years before.

I soon settled back into RAF base life and met a couple of WRENS who were also stationed out there called Julie and Karla. They were really enjoying the travelling they got to do and enthused happiness, had I been qualified I might have been tempted to re-apply to join up. The camaraderie in the forces has to be experienced to be understood, they become family to each other and I can see why ex servicemen and women find it difficult to adjust back to Civvy Street where it is every man for himself.

Gill and Craig were loving being in Malta, Craig worked in air traffic control and so was at work most days. We spent the days out and about and most evenings in the social club. I went out with a Maltese chap called Greg for the fortnight I was there and he took me to some of the less touristy beaches and we played tennis in ninety degrees of heat. Gill and I talked late into the night every night, she would reminisce about her nursing days and we would compare notes. The children seemed happy and settled into their new life and school. I also caught up a bit on news of Gill's brother who intrigued me, he was an actor, a struggling actor really who had mainly acted in commercials so far but his life fascinated me anyway.

Craig showed me round air traffic control and it was fascinating to see the monitors with aeroplanes shown as little moving dots. I wasn't allowed to speak to any of the controllers at the monitors because they had to concentrate but Craig explained how it all worked and the safe distances between planes that they had to maintain. Incredible really with the speed of fighter jets and I could see how stressful the job could be as the lives of these pilots were in the hands of the air traffic controllers. The fortnight went far too quickly and Gill, Craig and the poor besotted Greg took me to the airport for my flight home.

Another patient on the orthopaedic ward was Bill who had been in a car accident and tragically, his girlfriend who was in the passenger seat had been killed outright, he had a broken leg but most of the damage was going on in his head and he wouldn't talk about it. Alas, accidental deaths were not uncommon as I have already mentioned and he certainly wasn't the only one I would come across with survivor guilt.

As a mere novice I never mentioned his girlfriend as I had been told in handover not to, this was in the days before counsellors and I am not sure how he ever came to terms with what had happened. Some days he would be happy and jokey, other days he would be dark and brooding, sometimes he could be a real pain. I was really hurt one day when he snapped.

'Just go away Dawn,' for no apparent reason. Obviously, now I see in retrospect that he was in shock and grieving plus all the guilt mixed in and he needed psychological help. I think he was seen by a psychiatrist but his needs were way beyond me as a newcomer but I felt for him, being a similar age. These were the feelings and dilemmas that I either came to accept because I was human or harden to them as some nurses and medics advocated. I didn't feel the latter was very helpful to either nurses or patients but many of the tragic situations a nurse comes across have to be dealt with in a way that maintain a level of compassion while not being overwhelmed by the experience.

One such experience happened one morning, a young man aged twenty five had been admitted the day before with multiple fractures following a car accident. One of the nurses noticed he had a rash on his chest and he complained of breathlessness, she called the doctor over. Within minutes this young man collapsed and the 'Crash' team were called. Tragically he didn't make it in spite of everyone's best efforts and it later turned out he had a rare complication following severe fractures called a fat embolism. Events like this are extremely rare and most nurses' I have spoken to have never come across this condition. When they do occur though, they affect everyone on a shift.

I would somehow learn to laugh and cry while

also trying to grow up myself, remember I was only eighteen myself and coming across traumas that most people may not ever come across in a lifetime. There were certainly nights when I cried myself to sleep over the suffering I was witnessing and times when I felt very much older than my years.

Sometimes laughter and jocularity helped diffuse some of the tension and it's easy to judge health care professionals for doing this but they cannot always take the weight of a person's world upon themselves or they would not survive and they might be caring for forty people who need to feel that they are the only person the nurse is dealing with that day. Giving of oneself is part of the role though and the best nurses are able to empathise with patients in a way that is unique to the patient without falling apart or being aloof. The worst kind of nurse is the one who does not feel at all, I have always wondered why such people stay in the job. Balance is not always maintained and as I said, I have cried my heart out on many occasions. I have also been angry, sad, scared and happy sometimes all in one day.

An example of one of the ironic, slightly humorous situations but still tragic happened to me while I was on the orthopaedic ward. It was mid afternoon and I was fairly near the balcony area when I heard a massive crash and a loud thump. I went out onto the balcony and saw a man on the floor outside. I opened the doors to see if he was alright thinking he had come from our ward, I heard a commotion above me. I looked up and saw that from the ward above, nurses and patients were looking down through a very big smashed window. It turned out the man, suffering from schizophrenia heard a voice that had told him to jump out of the window. He ended up being admitted to our ward with a fractured hip and multiple leg fractures. This was a bit of an extreme way to get admitted we laughed.

During one's nursing career it would be impossible to avoid meeting a 'groper' and this nurse was no exception. The groper always managed to have a hand where it shouldn't be when you tried to lift or move him or in fact, do anything to him. Men like this took special handling, I was to learn. First one had to incapacitate the hands in some way prior to any procedure, sometimes this was done by getting them to participate if possible and use their hands for assistance. Others had to be more forcefully disengaged in some way without causing harm. Yet others had to have a lecture from Sister. I remember one such occasion.

'Now Mr Smith, please keep your hands to yourself and let the nurses do their job.' To which Mr Smith denied all accusations, saying,

'Of course Sister, but it was an accident' and then he started all over again as soon as Sister's back was turned. Mr Smith certainly did not get a warmed bedpan.

Jim was a young teenage boy who had a rare liver cancer and would never leave the ward. Getting to know Jim was one of the defining moments of my career. While most young women were having fun or being bored at work or university, I was growing up fast in a world where families had to come to terms with unimaginable grief and where a young lad was never going to reach the age of eighteen.

One day, I was behind the curtains with Jim, who had never been told his diagnosis although I think he knew.

'Dawn.' He said, 'Can I ask you something?'

'Yes of course.' Please don't ask me your diagnosis, I was thinking as I would have to be evasive or I would get the sack.

'Can I touch your breast?' He asked in such an innocent, non lecherous way, I am not sure whether I blushed but I'm sure I did, I was obviously a little bit taken aback.

'I'm sorry Jim, I can't let you do that.' I managed to say, amazingly I was neither offended, shocked nor flattered. I moved the conversation on somehow. This simple request has stayed with me over the years; here was a young man who probably knew he was going to die, he was expressing his sexuality in the only way he knew how. It was a poignant moment which still leaves me with a deep sadness, a moment in time between a nurse and a patient but really just between a boy and a girl. I sat with him for a bit and we talked about other things, I just wanted to let him know that I wasn't angry or offended and we could still be friends but it would have been wrong for me to agree to his request.

I loved that boy more than words can express but it was a compassionate love and an admiration for the way in which he coped with being in hospital for so long and I am sure he was aware that he would not leave the ward alive as he was getting weaker and weaker by the day. He was virtually unable to do anything for himself and needed constant care. His family visited every day and one can only imagine the traumas they were going through, trying to put on a brave face and laugh and joke when their world was being turned upside down. Not enough is said about the pain and suffering families and friends go through but there is a lot more support now for them than there ever was in the 1970's. Nurses' were not really prepared for these kind of situations, we just had to dig deep into our humanity and try to come up with the best responses, sometimes they were right and sometimes they were wrong.

I gave my first injection to a patient while on the orthopaedic ward, we had practiced on oranges in training school.

'Oranges,' said Mrs Butcher, 'are the closest thing to human skin.' We tittered as we did at every opportunity and then began practicing. It was not easy to inject an orange I can tell you and the needles seemed enormous, in fact they were enormous, most intramuscular injections were given with a very long needle, those needles are only used for drawing up injections now and a shorter one is used to inject. We spent ages trying to inject these oranges, water would splash back, needles would bend.

'Ouch,' yelled Grace as she stabbed herself, 'Crikey, I'm going to bleed to death,' she complained as the blood poured from her finger, the needles were very sharp but not that sharp, Grace had a tendency to overreact.

'Don't worry,' said Sue, 'I'll go and get Nick for you.' Nick was the latest doctor that Grace had fallen in love with although she was still going out with Greg, a medical student.

'He is gorgeous isn't he?' Crowed Grace who then forgot all about bleeding to death and treated us to half an hour of her love woes. How was she going to tell Greg that she had met Nick? All this while the rest of us were trying to inject oranges, it was nauseating really but we were always interested in the next instalment of Grace's love life. Sue had a long term boyfriend back home in Manchester and Charlie and Bette were more interested in their studies, which is why we knew they would go far, I was more interested in my social life than studying but loved nursing, taking to it like a duck to water.

Mrs Butcher persevered with the oranges lesson and explained that needle-stick injuries were a relatively common occupational hazard for a nurse and to beware of the dangers of acquiring blood borne infection from contaminated needles. It was mainly hepatitis B that was known about then but a new deadly virus was to be discovered in the early 1980's that was to change everything, the dreaded HIV virus which could lead to AIDS. Things have moved on a long way to try to protect nurses, doctors and phlebotomists from these infections among others. HIV and AIDS was not discovered when I first started training, it emerged in the early 1980's when gay men and drug users were mainly diagnosed with the condition. It probably was around in the late 1970's though as it spread in the 1980's across the continents and attracted more interest and fear when it was diagnosed in heterosexual people.

Nurses were at high risk of needle stick injuries as for many years' doctors were under the impression that it was a nurse's job to clear up trolleys after them, I found this particularly common in midwifery. The doctor would leave contaminated needles and other sharps on a trolley covered in blood, remove their gowns and gloves and leave the room, it was a very high risk practice as the midwife would have to peel back cloths and swabs to find the needles and dispose of them safely. It was quite rightly challenged by the Senior Midwife, Jackie, who frogmarched the doctors back into the room to dispose of their own sharps explaining to them that other staff' were not there to clean up after them.

Most doctors who were new to the labour ward tried it on.

'Sorry Sister, I have to go to theatre.' Dr Bates declared and he dashed off the labour ward. When he came back three hours later Jackie took him into a labour room.

'There is your trolley doctor, clean it up.' She said and marched off. The sheepish doctor did as he was told and learned his lesson as did all of them who worked with Jackie. Many nurses have had at least one needle-stick injury and we are just thankful that the majority of patients do not carry serious infections but it is an occupational hazard in spite of all the safeguards, I have had numerous sharps injuries over the years and I am not generally clumsy but long shifts, high stress levels mixed with multiple interruptions make the incidents inevitable at some stage. Perhaps the government might take this into account when deciding that nurses should work until they are ninety nine, or perhaps they hope that we will pick up some infectious disease that will kill us off shortly after retirement to save pension costs.

In order to give my first injection I was to jab a poor patient who had kindly given his permission. I take my hat off to all of the brave patients I have met over the years who stoically said.

'They've got to learn somehow, it might as well be on me.' There was a lot to remember – most of our injections would be given intramuscularly into the gluteus maximus muscle. I trained in the days of 'see one, do one, teach one', that applied to both doctors and nurses and I knew that once I had done this first one under supervision that would be it.

'Now,' I remembered Mrs Butcher saying, 'once you have checked you have the right patient (good point), break the ampoule, draw up the injection with a needle, discard, then attach a new needle, expel any air, draw an imaginary line dividing the buttock into four, swab the area and give your injection into the upper, outer quadrant in order to avoid hitting the sciatic nerve (equally good point as this could cause severe damage), make a quick motion with the needle, draw plunger back to ensure you are not in a blood vessel and then inject the solution, withdraw the needle and wipe area with a swab ensuring it has stopped bleeding before you leave then re-sheath (an absolute 'no-no' now) the needle and dispose of the syringe, needle and ampoule into a sharps container.'

Most of the drawing up and drug checking was done in the medical room with the staff nurse who was supervising. This was perhaps as well because the first ampoule I crushed to smithereens. Second attempt went well though and off we went to the bedside with all the equipment drawn up and placed in a stainless steel kidney dish (so called because of the shape). The patient was very helpful and reassuring, an older man who kept smiling and telling me I would be fine. Off he went onto his side saying.

'Go on nurse,' while Staff Nurse said,

'Hurry up nurse I've got loads to do,' and then with trembling hands I picked up the syringe, and by rote followed Mrs Butcher's instructions in my head, my stab probably wasn't as confident as it could have been and I think the needle went in and out twice but other than that, sweaty palms and face aside it went rather well. The staff nurse was pleased and the man kindly said he didn't feel a thing, although I did see him rubbing his behind later when he thought I wasn't looking. I can honestly say though, that injecting human skin felt nothing like orange peel but I didn't have the heart to tell Mrs Butcher.

I was soon to learn that the camaraderie of hospital life was important and working together with other student nurses during the formative years was something special. Training wasn't carried out in universities at the time and I have often wondered if I missed out on the university experience but when I think about nurse training and the fun we had on the wards, the doctors mess parties and the social life I don't think I missed out all that much. I later studied at university and have taught in a few and personally I think going to university should come with a Government Health Warning.

Alas, my time on male orthopaedics came to an end and although I was still very new, I had learnt so much on my first placement. There was a huge bit of excitement before I left when one day, out of the blue, one of my colleagues went to take Mr Graham his dinner and he said thank you. There was a huge clatter as she dropped the tray on the floor in her excitement. The whole ward was in uproar as Sister was called and then the doctors. Nobody could disguise the joy they felt that this man had regained his speech spontaneously. We were all talking about miracles for days.

I said a fond goodbye to the staff nurse who had been really helpful and to Jim who had not died during my time which I was glad about. On the day I left a group of the lads who had been let loose from traction, braved using their walking sticks and walked me off the ward to say goodbye and thanks, it was a nice gesture and I appreciated it. I was making it though and couldn't wait to get on with the rest of my training.

Chapter 6

Medical Ward - Early Mornings and Late Nights

During training I worked on both male and female medical wards. As a young nurse I was told that men were easier to nurse than women due to the fact that they still tried to maintain an element of manliness and therefore were considered less whiney. I can't say that I noticed any real difference and I have met both brave and tender souls in both sexes. Medical wards are hard work, patients are ill and some of the illnesses are horrendous. Conditions range from asthma to cancer and everything else in between. There were larger proportions of elderly people on medical wards due to the nature of the illnesses and before the days of 'no lifting' the work was both physically and mentally taxing.

It was always important to keep patients' moving to prevent pressure sores and deep vein thrombosis and so the days were filled with shifting people up beds using various lifting techniques, getting them in and out of bed, turning and generally manhandling them. Patients would call out.

'Hurry up nurse, I need to sit up, go to the toilet, use a bedpan, change position,' or whatever. We would then arrive in twos say.

'Right Mrs ....., up we go.' Before you knew it we would have one knee on the bed either side of the patient, shoulders under their armpits and they would fly up the bed if they were light and if they were heavier they might move two inches. This lift was called the 'Australian'. There were others of course but this was a favourite for moving people up beds.

Lifting people from the floor to the bed or out of chairs and baths was also common practice when I trained. Nurses, like patients, come in all shapes and sizes and so there would be short, size tens like me (wish I was still that size), lifting with taller and bigger sized nurses. It is worse for the taller people as they have further to bend when lifting with someone shorter and so bad backs were more common for them. The beds were steel framed with a back rest that pulled out and that was the sum total of technology applied.

Nowadays the beds go up and down at the push of a button but in the 1970's this was not the case, for me a Shorty the beds were too high and for taller people they were too low. Many nurses ended up damaging their backs and this would be a major cause of sickness. Sickness had other causes too mainly under the heading of viral illness and these included late nights, family gatherings and parties. Back problems were later tackled when moving and handling regulations were introduced and while some of the legislation is just plain silly, it was meant to have a major impact on protecting nurses and anyone else in the workplace from what commonly ended up as lifelong back pain, however, some would argue that it has had very little impact and that it has just shifted the type of back injury healthcare professionals acquire.

The first medical ward I worked on was female (before the days of mixed wards) and also a Nightingale ward. It was incredibly busy and I met some lovely patients. Janet was twenty six years old and had been admitted with abdominal pain, bleeding and diarrhoea, she was diagnosed with Crohn's disease. This is a condition that develops usually in young people between the ages of fifteen and thirty five, it is an inflammatory bowel disease although the inflammation can occur anywhere in the digestive system from the mouth to the anus.

Janet's symptoms were typical of the disease with crampy abdominal pains, watery diarrhoea and weight loss, she had been frightened she might have cancer but barium enema and blood tests had confirmed the Crohn's diagnosis. Although relieved that she didn't have cancer she now had to come to terms with the fact she had a chronic bowel disease with embarrassing symptoms for a young woman. Janet explained she had been having symptoms of diarrhoea, sometimes up to ten times a day for about six months, she had stopped going out because she never knew when the pain and diarrhoea would occur, she had been too embarrassed to go the her doctor and had hidden herself away in her one bedroom flat making excuses not to go out with friends.

She worked in an office and although she tried to hide the need to go to the toilet so often, others had noticed, she had become really worried about smells and wind which accompany the disease and was just about to quit her job when one of the girls in the office had befriended her and explained she had a cousin with similar symptoms. Thankfully this friend encouraged her to visit a doctor and he sent her into hospital for investigations. Diagnosis was just the first step in her journey to coping with living with this condition and she would have to learn to juggle medication to control the diarrhoea, pain relief and courses of steroids for flare ups. Janet seemed to be coping well until one day a young man appeared on the ward.

'Can you tell me where to find Janet Ross?' He asked, I pointed out the bed where Janet was and watched him go down the ward. I could see her look of horror when she saw him and was just about to go and ask him to leave when she burst into tears, he put his arms around her and she cried and cried on his shoulder. I went towards them and seeing they were now talking, I closed the curtains to give them a bit of privacy. Later when I spoke to Janet, she told me the story.

'I met Jake when I was twenty three on a holiday in Spain, he lives in London and we went out together, seeing each other at weekends and for holidays, just when all these symptoms started he took me out to a posh restaurant in Covent Garden and proposed. I was really excited and said yes but then the symptoms got worse, I began to think I had a serious illness and because of the diarrhoea I kept putting him off coming to Leicester and I kept cancelling going to London. Finally we had a row, he said I didn't love him anymore and thought I was seeing someone else, I told him we needed to finish and he stormed off back to London.'

They had both been miserable ever since and would never have seen each other again if he hadn't phoned her mother the day before coming to visit to ask if Janet had found someone else. Her mother told him the full story and he was devastated that he had not tried to find out what was worrying Janet and so he took a day off work and travelled to Leicester the next day. Needless to say, Jake became a rock in Janet's recovery, supporting her every step of the way. Finally Janet was discharged and Jake collected her, they had got engaged again and hopefully the relationship succeeded in spite of her illness.

A few years later I was at a night club in London with one of my flatmates and met a guy called Lance who asked me out. He lived in Sussex and he invited me to spend a day visiting the sights such as Chichester Cathedral, we were both interested in photography and I still have some amazing photos from that day out. Lance seemed a bit on edge all day and I thought this was because he was nervous about our first date. We went back to his flat and then he told me his story. He too had Crohn's disease, diagnosed when he was twenty two, he was now thirty, unfortunately his disease wasn't helped by medication and he had ended up with surgery and an ileostomy.

An ileostomy brings out a loop of the small intestine through an opening in the lower abdomen, faeces are then passed through this opening into a bag. Because the waste doesn't reach the large intestine it tends to be very runny and quite offensive smelling. Lance had obviously been devastated by this surgery and he thought that going out with a nurse would help but it was quite obvious that he was very bitter about it and the affect it had on his sexuality.

To be honest, this was all a bit too much for me and probably for him on a first date and we parted at the end of the day without any plans to see each other again. I have found this quite common at times, men ask a nurse out because of some hidden agenda, obviously for some it is due to watching too many 'Carry On' movies but for others it can be similar to the one with Lance. What Lance needed was counselling to help him overcome his problems and then to find a girl similar to Janet's Jake. The last thing I wanted after caring for ill people all day was to go home to someone wanting a nurse. Dealing with what life hands out is one thing but this would have been something else, I liked to pride myself on the fact that if I was asked out it was because someone liked me or found me attractive not because of my job.

Constipation was and still can be a common reason for admission to a medical ward and the treatment then was a soap and water enema. Mrs Johnson had been transferred to the ward with constipation and was in a lot of pain, writhing about the bed. It was time for me to give my first enema. Off I went to collect all the equipment on a trolley, incontinence sheets, long thick rubber tubing, connectors, a funnel, K-Y Jelly, a jug of tepid water and the container of green soap.

At the bedside I explained to Mrs Johnson what was going to happen.

'Now Mrs Johnson, don't worry, we are just going to give you a 'little' enema (there was nothing little about it!). Once the fluid is in, you need to try and hold onto it for as long as possible and you'll feel better in no time.' I was really proud to be able to use the 'we' word. With Mrs Johnson on her left side, I was donned in big plastic apron and gloves looking something like a pathologist out of Morse and so it was time to proceed. A funnel was connected to one end of the tubing which was attached together with plastic connectors which often came apart during the procedure soaking many a nurse and many a bed, K-Y jelly was applied to the other end of the tubing and this was passed into the rectum, then came the soap and water mixture. No sooner was it in than it was out again, all sorts of noises were emitted with each passage of greeny, brown coloured water.

Trying to reassure Mrs Johnson and myself that this was just a simple procedure was harder than I thought. When we were taught how to do this and I had seen others do it, it hadn't had quite the same dramatic effect, some leakage but not a shower. Staff Nurse Baines soon realised that I had been a little over cautious in my insertion of the tubing and it was only half an inch inside. She helped me to push the tube a bit further in and while there were still some emissions it was more like a trickle than a torrent. Obviously still a nurse in the making and not totally confident or competent yet.

I am pleased to say though, that this is another procedure that is no longer practiced and enemas are now minute in comparison, compare Mount Everest with an ant hill and you will get the gist. Just a note on the old incontinence sheets that were meant to protect the bed from all sorts of leakages, well they just didn't. They were disposable and made up of plastic covered in what looked like papier mache. They held hardly any fluid and would move and disintegrate under patients' bottoms. Sheets would still have to be washed permanently unless about four incontinence sheets were used in one bed and even then the liquid would make its way onto the bed. The only useful thing at the time were the sheets of plastic covered with a draw sheet that covered the central part of the bed where a patient would sit but even these were not fool proof. Millions of pounds around the country must have been wasted on products that were of very little use.

Sometimes when I went home at night I wondered if I was living on the same planet as my non-nursing friends. Jackie worked in an insurance office and would tell me all about people's car accident claims and the annoying people she had spoken to that day and what the girls in the office were up to. I didn't dare talk about half the things I had come across in a day, partly because I wanted to forget about hospitals and illnesses, I found that while I loved my job, I wanted to keep it separate from my home life and most things were confidential anyway so I couldn't go into detail even if I wanted to. Jackie was also very prim and would not have wanted to hear about the wards. I had my nurse friends who I socialised with to discuss work with and it suited me to compartmentalise. Jackie had a boyfriend called Bill and I really disliked him when we first met but we later became the best of friends, keeping in touch long after he and Jackie split up.

One nurse friend I made was called Betty, she had long black hair and was a second year student nurse working on the same ward as me, we always had a laugh and she was good fun. Her background was very middle class but in nursing we were all equal. We used to play tennis as there were courts not too far from the hospital in Victoria Park, she had obviously learnt to play tennis at school and started off much better than me although being the competitive person I was, I soon got the hang of it and though I say it myself I had a great serve for one so small. It was a great way to unwind after an early shift in particular and eventually the matches became more equal although I lost most of them. When I got tired of losing we would play badminton where I always won.

Mrs Brownlee had bowel cancer and I had got to know her quite well, she was just thirty eight years old with three young children aged eight, six and four, she was in a bed next to Mrs Blake, a patient with ulcerative colitis and who prided herself on being a palm reader. Thankfully, Mrs Brownlee didn't have her palm read, she fought so bravely and I never once found her feeling sorry for herself, we always had a laugh and joke. We kept in touch for a few years until she finally lost her fight with the dreadful disease and died. Mrs Blake did insist on reading my palm and told me I would go very far in my career, I did move to London! Another patient who told me I would go far was a patient who worked as a barrister.

Mrs Bremner was admitted with liver cirrhosis aged sixty six, her lifetime of drinking had caught up with her and on admission she looked at least eighty years old, thin, gaunt with very yellow skin, she looked as if she had been abroad but not in a healthy way at all. Her face was full of worry lines and she was barely conscious. The doctors had put up an intravenous infusion and she had been given intravenous diazepam to try to reduce the drink tremors she had during her arrival to A&E. She was transferred to us mid afternoon on a very busy 'on take' day when we took emergencies from the A&E department and transfers from Intensive Care Unit. I was the admitting nurse.

'Hello Mrs Bremner, my name is Nurse Brookes.' During admission I was supposed to have a chat with the patient about the ward, how they were feeling, take a medical and social history, write it all down and then do a full set of observations, check the drip (IV infusion), make sure she had all the relevant charts and make her comfortable. I was getting nowhere fast, I had drawn the curtains around to ensure we had the customary privacy and was trying to get her to talk but she was very sleepy from diazepam. I was writing out as much as I could from the notes sent from casualty when she finally woke up.

'Where am I?'

'You are in the Royal Infirmary, my name is Nurse Brookes'

'What's your proper name?' she asked

'Dawn, I said but don't let Sister hear you call me by my first name or I'll be in trouble'

'How did I get here', she spoke with quite a posh accent, I realised that this surprised me as I thought all alcoholics were rough people, no idea where I got that idea from, I can't say it was my specialist subject.

'Your sister found you unconscious and called for an ambulance.' I answered.

'I bet she did,' she half smiled and I didn't know whether she was angry or pleased, 'Is there anything to drink around here?' she continued.

'I can get you water, tea or coffee?'

'Flip,' she muttered then continued. 'How long have I been here?'

'On this ward about thirty minutes, you were in Casualty all night and most of today. Do you mind if I ask you some questions?'

'Ask away,' she said, then fell asleep. I continued with the charts, asked if I could do TPR & BP to which she grunted consent; checked her IV and when the next bag change was due. Intravenous fluids were always written up on an IV fluid chart and we had to work out the rate in drops per minute and manually count how many drops were being released, we needed to regularly check that drips were not going through too fast or too slow as they were often temperamental. Too fast and the patient would get fluid overload and could end up in serious trouble with heart failure or worse if potassium was in the IV fluid, too slow and the patient would get dehydrated if they were not taking other fluids by mouth. Some patients were admitted Nil by Mouth and had a sign above the bed to warn us and relatives not to give them food or drink.

I was familiar with drip bags from my time working at Travenol Laboratories and during my nursing I changed hundreds of drips. Once a drip had gone through air could pass into the tubing making it difficult to put up the next bag as the air had to be flicked back up the tube until it was all gone otherwise gravity from the next bag would cause air to enter the veins which was obviously dangerous. More often than not blood would flow back through the tubing from the cannula in the arm and this would then clot and the drip would no longer work and a doctor would have to be called to re-site it, being none too pleased about it. We also had to check the entry site as some would become infected or the cannula would move and the fluid would enter the surrounding skin, the drip would then have 'tissued' and would have to be stopped and re-sited. I checked the site and all was well but on picking up the scrawny, yellow arm I felt sad for this woman who was more than likely going to die here. I had read her history and saw that she had been fit and well until she lost her daughter in a car accident when she was thirty, after that her marriage broke up and she had taken to the bottle. There wasn't a lot of sympathy for alcoholics in the NHS at the time and A&E staff were not usually kind to them when they were admitted.

Trying to punish an alcoholic, sadly just reinforces their own self belief that they are worthless which I think just perpetuates an already vicious cycle. I have met many alcoholics and drug addicts during my career and although they can be manipulative and dishonest in order to feed their habit, I have found that kindness can and does result in lifestyle change.

I completed all the relevant charts noting that Mrs Bremner also had a urinary catheter in place, I went to the sluice to find a catheter stand and fixed the catheter to the stand and placed the stand on the floor, checking the catheter was draining. Six months into training and I was feeling very skilled, not so when I first encountered a catheter on male orthopaedics but that all seemed a long time ago. I was on a late that night and went to see Mrs Bremner before going off duty to see if she would like anything.

'No thanks, I think I'll just go to sleep, I feel very tired.' She said and I turned to leave. 'Dawn' she called after me, 'Thank you, I am sorry you have seen me in this state, I wasn't always like this you know.'

'I know,' I said and squeezed her hand, 'Goodnight, see you tomorrow.' When I came in the next morning Mrs Bremner had died in the night, her sister came in to collect her things, she looked devastated. What a tragic end to a life, I thought and felt utterly helpless not for the first time since starting nursing.

Hospital terminology was a language by itself, there were so many things to learn without all the abbreviations. Some were straightforward but others not so. IV for instance was fairly easy, standing for intravenous but then there was IVP, IVI, IVC and so on. There were hundreds if not thousands of abbreviations and they would take up a book all by themselves.

The 'lates' and 'earlies' were catching up on me, it was a trying time, trying to study, working all hours, trying to keep up with my social life and I wasn't the only one feeling it. One day when I went to meet some of the others in my set for a break it seemed we were all nearing breaking point and we were only halfway through our first year.

'I can't take this anymore.' Complained Grace, 'I'm so tired all the time and I hate the ward I am on, Barker is a sadist' (Staff Nurse Baker, renowned for barking out orders), 'whose one aim in life is to make me look small, especially when there are doctors around.' Knowing how much Grace loved doctors I could feel her pain, I couldn't remember which one she had on the go at that moment.

'What sort of things is she doing to upset you?' I asked, by this time Bette and Sue had joined us and they looked just as cheesed off as we did.

'Sister asked me to pass a naso-gastric tube on a patient who was admitted with a stroke and couldn't swallow, it was my first one,' she managed a smile of excitement at this point, 'but then she sent Barker to supervise, well she might as well have sent Jack the Ripper, it couldn't have been more frightening. She hates me, as soon as we went into the treatment room and I started setting up the trolley she was snarling.'

'That's not right Nurse Tanner, you've forgotten the K-Y.' This was used to lubricate the tube to make it easier to be passed through the back of the nose and past the larynx into the oesophagus.

'I hadn't forgotten, she just wouldn't give me time to set it up before she started criticising, I was going through the list Mrs Butcher had taught us and how we'd set up in PTS, I was also trying to remember from the last one I'd seen Julie, the third year do, but no, Barker, or should I say Jack wouldn't let me think. She kept tutting and looking at her watch.'

'At this rate Nurse the patient will have died of starvation before we get there.'

'I finally got the trolley ready, gave Barker one of my fiercest looks and marched out of the treatment room to the patient. I ignored Barker completely and introduced myself to the patient explaining what I would be doing and then Barker interrupted.'

'Good morning, Mrs Askill, I am Staff Nurse Baker and this is Pupil Nurse Tanner, I am here to supervise the procedure and make sure it is done correctly by the trainee nurse,' she sneered, 'If you are not happy at any point please squeeze my hand and I will take over, is that OK?'

Grace was nearly in tears at this point. 'The patient did manage to nod and then she looked at me sympathetically even though she was the one who had had a stroke. I wanted to hug her and thank her and I was determined to get it right in spite of Barker. God must have heard my prayer because at this point Sister Mason came in and said that Barker needed to go and do the medicine round and that she would supervise. The whole atmosphere changed and Sister introduced herself, even Mrs Askill looked more relaxed.' Grace was laughing now and was coming out of her morose state, the caffeine was starting to kick in as well.

'Well, what was it like?' We all chanted in unison as none of us had carried out this procedure on a real patient yet.

'It went really well, Mrs Askill was brilliant at not getting too tense and after the second attempt it was in the stomach, it was so exciting, I aspirated with a syringe like we'd been taught and squirted a small amount on blue litmus paper and it turned pink so I knew it was in the stomach. Sister was delighted and told the patient how good I was to which she nodded and then I was allowed to give her the first feed. Adrian came up to me afterwards and said I was a star.'

Now I remembered, Adrian was the latest flame, a senior medical student in his final year.

'I'm so jealous.' Sue sighed and then frowned, this was so unusual, we all looked at her.

'What's the matter?' asked Bette.

'Graham finished with me last night, he said it was too difficult with us being apart and that he had met someone else. The worst thing was I only had enough change to hear this before my money ran out and so didn't even get to finish the conversation. I thought we were so happy, I thought we would marry.' At this point the tears flowed and we could see from her swollen eyes this wasn't the first time she had cried. We were stunned, they had indeed seemed the perfect couple, they had met at school and been dating since they were sixteen, Sue hadn't even looked at another guy since starting training and had gone home to Manchester whenever she could although it was difficult with shifts and her boyfriend was at Manchester University studying History.

'I can't believe it!' Said Bette, 'what a b..........'

'I know how you feel.' Grace sympathised, she had been through more than enough breakups already, although mainly of her own doing. 'There's a doctors mess party on Saturday night and you are coming,' she continued as if this would solve all ills and mend the broken heart we were witnessing.

'I think we should all go just for the sake of getting a drink and forgetting about work for a bit, we don't have to go looking for men.' I sent a warning glance over to Grace.

'That's true, we don't we will just have some girl fun and have a few drinks that should help. We are back in school on Monday so that will be great and I can celebrate never having to see Barker again.'

'Maybe,' said Sue, I was wondering whether to go home and have this out face to face but if he's met someone else I guess there's not much point and I don't want him to see me like this anyway or my parents.' My heart went out to her, she looked so sad, I had never experienced heartbreak in my relationships as I had always done the breaking up, I felt a bit guilty for a moment about the hearts I had probably broken but it didn't pay to dwell so I got up.

'Better get back to the ward, see you Saturday, I'll come to yours to get ready if that's alright?'

'Of course it is, why don't you sleepover, save you getting a taxi or worse still, walking?' Bette replied, they knew I was a terror for walking home late at night after the buses had finished and they worried I was going to be attacked one night. Sometimes I worried too but I'd rather walk home than not go out and I didn't have money for taxi fares. It was easier when I moved out of home and lived nearer to Charles Frears at least. I did always run up my street after walking home via the main roads, the worst bit was walking past Fosse Park and I always crossed over to the other side of the road in case anyone was lurking, thankfully no-one ever was.

The mess party was held in one of the downstairs rooms, we could hear the music blaring as we arrived, Dancing Queen by Abba greeted us as we walked into the room and we immediately felt like dancing, Grace spotted Adrian and disappeared in a flash.

'So much for a girly night!' Bette groaned, Sue still looked out of sorts which was hardly surprising, we helped ourselves to a drink from the makeshift bar, booze was always free at these parties as the doctors had more money than we did and stocked up before the party started. I had a glass of white wine in my hand and I could see Sue was getting close to tears as she noticed many people pairing up.

'Come on,' I said, 'let's dance', by now Elvis Presley's, Way Down was playing and so we found some space and danced around our handbags. Sue was drinking Bacardi & Coke, a drink that was popularised in the 1970's from people holidaying in Spain. It wasn't long before she was looking a lot better, well, maybe worse for wear was more like it but at least she was smiling. Bette was also getting merry and had attracted the attention of a houseman I recognised from orthopaedics.

I was refusing all offers as I knew Sue would end up in tears and I decided to be disciplined unless she accepted a dance offer but I knew that was unlikely unless she was out of her head which was not an impossibility with the way she was downing the Bacardi's. Sue was not really a drinker and a few hours and numerous drinks later she was rambling.

'I loved him, how could he do this to me? I hate him, I need to find a phone box and tell him how much I hate him.' She staggered off with me in tow,

'No, that's not a good idea' I said, anyway he

won't be home, it's Saturday night and he will be ....,' blast I shouldn't have said that.

'You mean he'll be out with a slut.' I didn't think that was fair on the new girlfriend but I wasn't going to argue.

'Well he might have gone home to see his parents.' I said weakly

'Yeh sure, I'll ring him there then, he needs to be told what a despicable pig he is.' That's about as strong as it got with Sue. Just then Bette joined us and realising I was in a fix, intervened.

'Come on, let's do the bump.' This was a popular dance of the 1970's involving swaying or jumping and bumping hips to the beat of the music, during the dance, girls would dance together or with boys. The locomotion was still popular then as well and the evening ended at around one o clock in the morning with this dance. By this time Sue was barely able to walk and so we decided to split a taxi, Grace suddenly appeared from nowhere and we made our way home. Sue was still rambling about making phone calls but she wouldn't have been able to dial a number so we just agreed with her. Grace was pretty far gone as well although thankfully, she and Adrian hadn't fallen out.

'I think I am in love.' She said but Bette and I shut her up before she started to wax lyrical and upset Sue even more.

'I had a good time tonight.' Said Sue, yes, great I thought as I had spent the whole evening playing nursemaid, I had behaved like Mother Theresa for the whole evening and was tired. We got to the flat and Sue promptly threw up all over their lounge.

Chapter 7

Crawly Things

Mr Jarvis was admitted to the ward I was working on, he was eighty and had been found on the floor at home. When he arrived I was the admitting nurse and so I went to assess him. I could see he was generally unkempt and had probably not washed in a very long time. Dirt was ingrained into his wrinkles and his skin, his face was round with eyes that protruded from his face, they didn't seem to fit I remember thinking. His hair was grey, although it looked black and he had scales of dandruff on his head. His fingernails were too long for a man and caked with dirt, his clothes were quite frankly ready for incineration. A musty smell surrounded him. When I had cautiously removed his jacket, shirt and vest and deposited them into a plastic bag, I decided a hospital gown was the most appropriate attire at this time as a bath was going to be needed almost immediately.

He had been to Casualty and they had excluded any broken bones, I don't think he had spent very long there unsurprisingly. Amazingly there was no evidence of fleas or head lice. I helped him take his trousers off and noticed he had really dirty crepe bandages covering both of his lower legs.

'Have you put these bandages on yourself Mr Jarvis?' I asked.

'Yes nurse, I look after myself you see.'

'Do you know when you last changed them?'

'Can't say I remember Nurse, I expect it was a while ago.'

Once I had helped him into a gown to protect his dignity, I decided I was going to need a dressing trolley. I was a bit more experienced now and could make these decisions for myself. I called one of my colleagues, another first year called Natalie, to assist and we went back to Mr Jarvis. As I started to remove the bandages there seemed to be some movement underneath, at first I thought this was my imagination but the more I removed the more there was movement. Finally I got them all off and both my colleague and I took two steps back, aghast, we stared at the sight in front of us. Hundreds of huge maggots (I remembered these from my fishing days), were busily wriggling around on the wounds, they seemed very well fed.

Natalie had already left way too quickly in my opinion, leaving me to take a big gulp, I smiled at Mr Jarvis and explained that I needed to fetch something, then, feeling quite sick I withdrew to a safe distance and called for Sister Garfield, noticing Natalie was nowhere to be found.

Sister came and took a look, behaving as if this was an everyday occurrence, I guess she had seen it all before, she took it in her stride.

'Mr Jarvis, you appear to have some visitors on your legs, maggots I believe.' Mr Jarvis' eyes protruded even further,

'I thought there was some nibbling going on

down there Sister.'

Sister turned to me, 'note how clean the wounds are Nurse Brookes, the maggots have cleaned all of the slough (dead tissue) away. Slough was really difficult to get rid of usually. Now just wash the maggots off and make sure they are all removed and disposed of, I don't want any loose on the ward and then clean the wounds with hydrogen peroxide and dress them with eusol and paraffin soaked gauze.' In later years, sterile maggots would become part of wound debriding for some patients and are now bred in sterile conditions solely for this purpose on a farm in Wales. They are expensive to buy in. Alan Sugar would be very impressed.

Funny things go on in farms in Wales, I heard that one of them was looking into the effects of dog saliva on wound healing. Hydrogen peroxide, eusol and paraffin would later be condemned for being caustic and damaging wound beds and is no longer used in wound treatment. This is one of life's little ironies, although we can't breed bluebottle maggots ourselves, thankfully. I am still not keen on maggots, but have used the safe, sterile ones on occasions. Mr Jarvis did get better and his wounds improved and we sent him home spick and span although I doubt he stayed that way for very long.

On the same ward I met Mrs Rafferty, a gypsy as they were known then, now I think she would be called a Traveller. Mrs Rafferty was admitted with a breast lump that had been found during a routine examination by a GP who visited the Gypsy camp to try to get people to register with his surgery. He was quite innovative in many ways as for years travellers received poor healthcare due to not being registered with GP practices and a general mistrust of authority. There are many programmes now set up to try to bridge this gap.

Mrs Rafferty was tiny, even in comparison to me, I think she was about four foot, ten inches and very thin. Her clothes had seen better days although they looked clean and generally she also looked clean. I handed her a nightdress to change into and explained I would be back to take some observations and ask some questions before the doctor examined her. When I went back, she looked even smaller, buried in the hospital nightdress with the gap at the back, I think, designed to make toileting easier. These hospital nightdresses were given to men and women and were often a source of amusement when patients' forgot to hold them together at the back, leaving bottoms very much exposed.

I explained I would be checking TPR and BP and she got onto the bed. As I reached to get the new thermometer that had been placed in the container behind the bed I was distracted by something I had seen in my peripheral vision. As I sheepishly looked in that direction I could see movement in her hair. I tried not to gasp and felt an irresistible itchiness come over my own head immediately. I managed to excuse myself for a minute and went to fetch Sister Garfield for the second time in the space of a few weeks.

'My, my Nurse we are having quite a month

aren't we?' She chuckled. Sister was again not at all phased by this turn up of events although she didn't get quite as close as she had to Mr Jarvis. 'Mrs Rafferty, have you noticed any itchiness in your head?' she asked.

'Well now you mention it, I have been a bit scratchy recently, is there a problem?'

'I'll just have a quick look.' Sister did have a very quick look indeed, briefly parting the hair. 'Oh yes, I see the problem, you have some unwanted visitors to your head, would you be ok with nurse applying some treatment in the bathroom?'

'That would be grand,' replied Mrs Rafferty. No it wouldn't I thought but having been treated by my mum when the nit nurse found nits at school on a couple of occasions, it was something I felt able to do, although not with my usual enthusiasm. I bought some solution on the way home and treated myself as soon as I got through the door and thankfully didn't get any visitors myself.

When working as a district nurse I once visited a home of a couple who could only be described as hoarders. I was in my car driving to the next patient with the window down, it was a beautiful, sunny day and I looked down and saw a flea on my arm. I had to make a slight detour for a shower and change before carrying on with my day.

Chapter 8

Ever Constant Jerry

Nurses like everyone, have people that are important to them and these people often provide the support needed at the end of a difficult shift and they also have to put up with the shift work which sometimes interferes with the ability to make plans. Jerry was one of the people who provided me with this kind of support during my training and he deserves a mention.

At the start of my second year I went out for a meal with Jackie and Bill. After going to a pub in town we would often stop on the way home at an Indian Restaurant on the High Street. It was a Thursday night and we were put on a table with a rowdy rugby crowd. I happened to be sitting next to one of them and we started talking. He was tall at around six foot, had dark black hair, brown eyes and was relatively handsome. He did have a bit of a beer belly and a beard and moustache which I didn't normally go for but he seemed a good sort, he introduced himself as Jerry and apologised for his rowdy mates. I noticed he wasn't smoking but he didn't seem to mind that we did (I gave up when I was twenty three). By the end of the meal he had asked me out and we arranged for him to collect me the following night from home.

Jerry became a long term boyfriend (long term

for me anyway) and we made up a foursome with Jackie & Bill for about a year. We were both still living at home, as was Jackie and Bill was the only one with a flat so we would often spend Saturday nights at Bill's. I later moved into my beloved bedsit on Holmfield Road, opposite Charles Frears, then Jerry was a regular at weekends.

The bedsit was not far from where Bill's flat was on Uppingham Road and Jerry lived in Oadby which was a few miles north. We went out to most places as a foursome for about a year and he was a great support throughout my training. He was a carpenter and earned a reasonable salary so we went out a fair bit, I was a bit less overdrawn while going out with Jerry. We would play tennis together and chat for hours, although he was relatively quiet for a rugby playing carpenter. He was basically a really nice lad with a good upbringing who was very polite. I think Bill got on his nerves a bit sometimes as he tended to be quite loud and a bit of a bragger. Bill was relatively small at about five foot, six, fair haired with a moustache, he wore metal framed glasses, was quite slim, about eight years older than the rest of us and definitely not good looking but he was someone I grew to like. Jerry put up with the shifts I worked and didn't complain too much when I worked most weekends and even put up with me working nights.

The two of us went on a camping holiday to France which was an experience as I had never been camping. Jerry had booked us on a hovercraft to Boulogne and amazingly there was a heat wave in the north of France. Jerry carried everything and we walked for miles and I got a bit too much sunburn. I still have a photo of him, walking along in the middle of nowhere looking like a packhorse. We took a train to Paris for the day but I don't think we had much time to spend there before having to get a train back to Boulogne as I don't remember seeing any of the main attractions. I am happy to say I went again a few years ago to celebrate a friend's fiftieth birthday and another friend's, daughter's eighteenth and we saw most of the sights, staying a short walk away from the Arch de Triumph and the Champs Elysees.

In spite of the shifts I still managed to have a good social life in that second year of training sometimes to the point of madness. One night when I was out with Jerry, Jackie and Bill in the Corn Exchange, a pub which was our local, we came up with one of those moments of madness ideas. I was on an early late that weekend so had finished at five fifteen and was not due to go into work until twelve thirty the next day which was a Sunday. I don't know who had the bright idea that we should drive to Skeggy (Skegness), a mere sixty miles away and go for a paddle in the sea but we all agreed to the plan. It was January and so the sea was probably not uppermost in the majority of peoples' minds, nevertheless we embraced the idea with gusto. We all bundled into Jerry's car and off we went. Jerry was pretty good at sticking to drink driving limits and as far as I remember had on this occasion. By the time we got to Skeggy it was about two o clock in the morning as there were no motorways that way and we were feeling a bit more tired than at the beginning of the journey and a bit less enthusiastic. We managed to find a car parking space near the beach, I'm joking, as you can imagine we were the only people there.

We ran onto the beach more to keep ourselves warm than through excitement and began a fairly cautious paddle. Before long the cold had woke us up again and I think I was the first one to be thrown into the sea which of course meant that we all ended up in the freezing cold North Sea. This was all very well but we didn't have any change of clothes with us, more importantly, no towels and once the laughing had stopped, the cold set in. We were frozen, wet and not a little hungry. It was now five o clock on a Sunday morning and back in 1978 there was no all night Asda and Sunday was still a day of rest for the majority of people so there was absolutely no chance of warming up anywhere or finding food and I had to be in work later that day. My enthusiasm was waning and so I suggested we go home.

The journey home was not as animated as the journey going and we were all shivering. Poor Jerry's car was soaked through from four wet human beings and in spite of the heating being on full blast all the way home we were barely dry when we made it. We got back at around eight o clock as the lack of motorways and Jerry's shivering made the journey rather slow. We all had breakfast at my place, the others soon felt better as they were all heading home for a long sleep. I decided it wasn't worth trying to sleep before going to work and went in at half past twelve, the rest of the day is a haze, the other three of course did go home to bed while I worked until nine thirty in the evening and then an hour's journey to get home. I slept very well that night after being up for over forty hours and would like to say I learned my lesson about not burning the candle at both ends but of course I didn't and there were a few more all nighters.

Jerry had proposed to me on more than one occasion and it was clear he was in it for the long haul. Sadly, I was never great at commitment and felt it would be unfair to him to keep him attached to me when he was so obviously the marrying kind. The inevitable time came for me to tell him we were finished which he did take quite hard. I felt I was too young to settle down and carried on feeling like this until I felt I was too old to change and so have maintained a happy single life to this day. I think if there had been anyone I would have married it was definitely the long suffering Jerry and I hope he is now happily married with oodles of children and grandchildren. Jackie and Bill also split up and Bill and I went out together (as friends) for a couple of years before I moved to London.

Another event stands out during my time with Jerry is one that stemmed back to my first love. When I was fifteen I fell in love with an eighteen year old lad called Joe. Joe used to hang out with black guys and even spoke like them which I always found a bit bizarre, he would say things with a West

Indian accent and they just didn't sound right coming from his mouth. I was attracted to him from the minute we met; he was fair haired, had the most gorgeous blue eyes and was very fresh faced. When he smiled my heart missed a beat, he had the most engaging smile I had ever seen in a boy.

He was always nice to me and treated me with respect, we had an unusual relationship as he never really asked me out, he was just there and we got on really well. The fly in the ointment was that he was into drugs. I didn't know this at first but later discovered he was addicted to LSD and amphetamines. I hadn't seen him for a while and then I started receive letters from a prison when I was seventeen, apparently he had tried to fly off a building but fortunately someone stopped him before he fell to the ground, he was jailed for possession and drug use. After he was released from prison he came to my house one night, fortunately my parents were out, we chatted and kissed, this was the closest we had been since we knew each other and he was now twenty. I walked him to the bus stop (bizarre I know) and he took me by surprise when he said.

'How would you feel about taking me on permanently?' Once I got over the shock of what I thought he was asking my head took over and before I knew it I was saying.

'I don't think I could handle it.' I was crazy about him and so it was with a very heavy heart that I amazed myself by saying this. He smiled that smile which made me kick myself and question whether I had heard him correctly. That was it; I didn't see him again. Why did I refuse? Well, I always felt my mum had made the wrong choice in her marriage and I had seen the consequences, I was determined not to make the same terrible mistake and so my head would always rule my heart (almost always anyway).

I had told Jerry all about Joe and had obviously put him on a pedestal which poor old Jerry could never quite live up to. How cruel we can be. One night we were in the Corn Exchange with some friends when suddenly we became aware of a horrible smell, we looked around and there on a seat next to us was a tramp. He was filthy and the smell was awful, we decided to leave and as we got up to go I had the shock of my life, I recognised this tramp as he looked up, it was Joe. He looked at me and behind all of the filth he still had those lovely appealing eyes that first attracted me to him.

'Take me home?' He asked quietly,

'I can't.' I replied and left with my friends. Everything in me wanted to go back and get him and sort him out but I knew deep down that this would not be possible. I left very quietly,

'Who was that?' Jerry asked and when I told him he retorted. 'So that's the wonderful Joe.'

'Mm,' I said, 'He's in a bit of a mess.'

'Yep!.' He said and put his arm around me, I have to say that Jerry was not the type to be unkind and rub it in. Why on earth didn't I marry him? Truth is I just didn't love him.

That meeting with Joe had a profound effect on

me and I have always had a soft spot for the homeless and addicts, perhaps tinged with guilt. They all have a history but have taken a few wrong turns along the way before ending up in the state they are in and 'but for the grace of God, there go I.' In all my dealings with alcoholics and drug addicts since then maybe there has been that bit of regret that I didn't help someone I thought I was in love with. When my head takes over though, I knew in my heart then and I know it now, there didn't seem a way back for Joe but maybe I'm wrong. Some things we will never know.

Chapter 9

The Final Gesture

It is inevitable in a nursing career that death is encountered and I came across death and dying on a fairly regular basis. When I began my nursing career death and dying nearly always took place in hospital. This trend came in with the medicalisation of almost everything which coincided to some extent with the break-up of the extended family as people moved further and further away from their roots, yours truly being an example of this.

I am not a sociologist and so do not pretend to comment from that point of view but in my experience this seems one of the most likely explanations along with that of hospitals actively encouraging the practice. Hospitals were not and even to this day are not equipped to deal with death and dying and patients did not always have a 'good death'.

Pain management was unsophisticated at the time and I frequently felt inadequate and anguished when faced with the suffering of some patients. I heard rumours from time to time that some doctors would have liked to overdose patients deliberately to reduce suffering but I never came across any evidence of this becoming a reality myself and whilst the newspapers do confirm this does happen from time to time I am sure it is very rare. I was often amazed at the strength people showed when faced with insufferable pain along with the prospect of dying.

Sometimes diamorphine injections were given with little effect and sometimes the effect was too much and a patient would be unable to communicate effectively with their loved ones. I remember sitting with an elderly man who was dying and who was in a lot of pain but he gritted his teeth and refused to cry out. I held his hand until a family member arrived and she told me he had been a mine clearer during the war. He had been brave in life and was going to be brave in death, she said. I could not stop the tears as I moved away from his bed and was more determined than ever to try and maintain standards in spite of the 'hurry up nurse' mentality of hospital life.

None of the problems associated with treatment were deliberate, it was mainly due to the knowledge base at the time and the constant battles with staffing levels on hospital wards. I can honestly say though, that no patient who we knew was dying, died alone, a member of staff was always allocated to a dying person if a relative or friend was not available, other staff members would rally round to cover the work so that a person could have a dignified death, something I hope still happens today in hospitals. The hospital chaplain or a priest or vicar from a patient's parish would usually visit to perform the last rites when a patient was near to death. We were always taught to ask a patient about their religion on admission and that spiritual needs should be addressed in the same way as physical ones. Where possible these needs were met and there was usually a hospital chapel available if patients wanted to attend a Sunday Service. The majority of patient's would declare themselves C of E or RC whether practising or not. Ministers from other religions were on a list held by the hospital reception and could be called in when needed.

Nowadays patients are moved out of hospital where possible to a preferable setting, be that home, a care home or a hospice if available. Things have moved on in relation to symptom control thanks to the hospice movement and many cancer charities, pain relief and palliative care is much improved and although end of life care for people with non-cancer diagnoses lagged behind for many years there has been a push in recent years to rectify this. More people end their lives at home or in hospices or specialised wards although hospitals still see a fair number of deaths as that last minute panic to call an ambulance is sometimes inevitable.

Laying a patient out was a procedure carried out when a patient died on a ward and administering this was a part of the training. It was always seen as the last kind gesture we could offer to a patient following death.

The inevitable day for me came when a female patient had died and we had to get the patient ready to go to the mortuary after the family had left. I went behind the curtain with a third year student nurse, called Josie, who was going to teach me how to carry out the procedure. Mrs Hadley was lying on her back with mouth and eyes open but there was that deathly stillness and pallor. This pallor changes very quickly to mottled blue, particularly when handling the patient. It has been reassuring for me over the years to note that what constitutes life, the soul if you have faith, departs at death. The light in the eyes has gone and to me, it seems that what is left is a shell as the person who was, is now gone. This was one of the first impressions I was left with on seeing a dead body.

I had been taught in class what to do but this is not quite as easy on a real person. We had been taught to speak to the person as if they were alive which took a bit of practice as I felt a bit daft at first. We were also taught to speak to unconscious patients as they may be able to hear what was said to them. With some nurses on hospital wards you are lucky if they speak to you when you are alive, let alone when you are dead. We had washed the front of Mrs Hadley's body when I pulled her towards me so that Josie could wash her back. I spoke to her as instructed.

'Mrs Hadley, I am just going to turn you towards me so that Nurse Blount can wash your back.' On doing so, Mrs Hadley let out an enormous groan and I jumped out of my skin, letting her go in the process. Josie was laughing at me.

What no-one had told me was that on moving a body the air that is still in the stomach can sometimes be emitted on movement which can make an unseemly noise as had happened to me. I eventually saw the funny side and we continued, albeit cautiously on my part. I paid great attention to Mrs Hadley in case she was still alive as I had read in books about people being buried alive but I think my imagination was getting the better of me, sadly she was indeed dead.

Laying out a patient involved a full wash and plugging the back passage with cotton wool which I always hated doing, it seemed undignified but it stopped any leakage of faecal matter. False teeth were put in the mouth which was then closed by tying a bandage from the chin to the head and tying at the top of the head, another procedure I really didn't like. A label was tied to the big toe for identification purposes. The patient was then dressed in a white plastic shroud and placed flat on their back. The body was finally wrapped in a sheet. Once finished, we called for the hospital porters to come and collect the body for the hospital morgue.

We closed all the curtains on the ward so that other patients would not see the awful metal morgue trolley. Of course the patients all knew what was going on although there was a conspiracy of silence and everything was done in hushed tones until the body had left the ward and normality resumed.

'Goodbye Mrs Hadley.' I said, shortly after, the noise and hustle and bustle returned, Josie and I finally stripped the bed, cleaned it and made it up ready for the next occupant who was waiting in the wings to move in.

Chapter 10

The Long Stand and other Procedures

It was during my time on a medical ward that I learnt about 'a long stand'. If a new student nurse was a bit of a 'know it all', she or he would be sent to a neighbouring ward for a long stand. Once arriving on the ward she would ask the ward sister for the long stand and would be told to wait there. After about ten minutes she would begin to think she had been forgotten and would ask another member of staff for the said stand and would be told to wait. After about thirty minutes the sister would return and tell the nurse to return to her ward.

'But I haven't got the long stand' she would protest. The sister would reply.

'You have had a long stand.' The nurse would then realise she had been had and hopefully return to her ward a bit red in the face and with a little more humility. Personally I never experienced anyone being sent for a long stand but I am assured it was common practice once upon a time. It may be one of those myths that exist in hospital folklore. Maybe I was always humble – I don't think. The Nursing auxiliaries swore these things really did happen though.

Another funny story I heard from a nursing auxiliary, was that a student nurse was asked to take a commode to a patient on bed rest which the nurse did. Shortly afterwards, the patient's head could be seen looking over the curtains. The nurse had placed the commode on the bed and sat the patient on it thinking that as he was on bed rest she shouldn't get him out of bed. There are many such hilarious stories and I am sure that some of them are true and some not so true but they make for interesting chats on night duty.

Some ward sisters were very helpful and some were just plain obnoxious. I had an experience with one of the latter while working on a medical ward. Sister Makin had a reputation for being a horror to student nurses. I had only been on the ward for a week when one of the doctors wanted to perform a lumbar puncture on a patient. The Sister called to me and said.

'Nurse Brookes, set up a trolley for a lumbar puncture.'

'I have never set up a trolley for a lumbar puncture sister.' I replied

'WELL LEARN!' She shouted and stormed off up the ward. I went into the treatment room and found a trolley, I was trembling and panicky. I just stared around at the multitude of cupboards wondering what on earth to do next. I was close to tears when Claire, the Staff Nurse came in. She was from Burnley

'What's up love?' I explained what had happened and she could see how upset I was. She showed me how to set up the trolley. After that I heard her tell Sister Makin she shouldn't have done that to me and Claire and I became firm friends for a number of years. Claire lived in the nursing home at the hospital and we would often share a bottle of wine at the end of late shifts and chat until late. Her boyfriend was a teacher who shared a house with friends and she would spend her days off with him. I got to know him quite well too and they later married although I think she still had to share with his housemates for a time after they were married.

As well as wine, Claire and I shared the same birthday, although she was a few years older than me. I lost touch with her when I moved to London to do further training but have fond memories of our friendship and am always grateful to her for rescuing me from the dreaded Sister Makin who I avoided like the plague for my whole stint on that ward. On qualifying I worked on the ward next to that one and Claire who by that time was the ward sister (the ogre had moved on) and I would meet for lunch in order to share stories and compare notes.

Some nurses, who were not familiar with anatomy, were sent to a nearby ward or to the medical room to find a Fallopian Tube which of course only existed within the female body but it was fun if a nurse did fall for this one, most didn't of course.

One Nursing Auxiliary told me about when she was nursing during the war and she had been out for the day on leave. Unfortunately she missed her last bus back to the hospital and telephoned Matron to let her know she would be late, this meant she was going to be in trouble when she got back the next day. On arriving back Matron called her into the office.

'I'm sorry I missed the bus Matron, I ran all the way to the bus stop but couldn't get there in time.'

'It's not that Miss Graham, I want to know why you were shouting at me.'

'Oh.' Finally the penny dropped. It had been the first time she had ever used a telephone and as she was fourteen miles away, she had thought she needed to make up the distance and had shouted at the top of her voice to Matron who had been almost deafened on the other end of the phone. We were in stitches at this story, imagining the scene and imagining poor matron with the phone in her hand. She explained this to Matron who saw the funny side of it, reprimanded her and let her go, I expect she chuckled afterwards.

Chapter 11

What's wrong with Decaffeinated Coffee?

Miss Wright had been admitted to the ward during the night with appendicitis and had been for surgery in the early hours of the morning. Before every shift we would have a handover and the night staff nurse got to Miss Wright.

'Felicity Wright, admitted last night with appendicitis, had appendicectomy at three o clock this morning, came back to the ward at five o clock, has had one pain killing injection in theatre. She's a barrister,' with this the Staff Nurse rolled her eyes to the sky to lots of sniggering. 'MISS Felicity Wright,' she continued in a dramatic tone, 'has also requested and is paying privately for a side room!' Now all of the staff were rolling their eyes. 'She can have sips of water for now and later in the day she can have full fluids and light diet.' The handover moved on to other patients on the ward. The issue for most of the nurses' was that of paying for a side room because this meant she could afford to be different. To me it was no issue at all, having been on a few forty bedded Nightingale wards now, if I could afford a side room, I would take it, as I am sure most of the nurses at handover would have too.

Most nurses who were unfortunate enough to be admitted to hospital automatically qualified for a side room out of professional courtesy so there was an element of hypocrisy here. The barrister bit obviously struck a chord for some too, this meant well educated and to some extent powerful. Nowadays nurses would ensure that she got the best care to make sure they didn't get sued as we live in a much more litigious climate. Personally while I understood the class barrier from both sides of the coin, it had never been a big thing. As far as I was concerned I would be friends with anyone who wanted to be friendly. In the case of nursing, I was there to do a job and one patient deserved the same attention as another. Obviously I liked some patients more than others but I would like to think that they would never be able to tell the difference, that was of course, a daily challenge.

Sometimes being in a side room had its disadvantages and it was easy to be ignored or forgotten with all the commotion happening on the ward. Miss Wright obviously had this experience as she hobbled out onto the ward, clutching her side. I saw her and went to assist her back to her room and ask what she wanted.

'Please may I have a cup of decaffeinated coffee?' She spoke like a member of the royal family. I had never heard such a posh accent. Patients in nearby beds also started doing the rolling eyes thing so I thought the safest thing was to assist her back to her room.

'I'll get you one.' I said, wondering where on earth I was going to get decaffeinated coffee from. Bear in mind this was the 1970's, it was not a common request.

'Oh thank you,' she replied and I was trying to ignore the guffaws going on around me. Hospital wards are boring for patients once they start to feel a little better and so this sort of thing was just what a few of the more mischievous ones were looking for.

'While you're at it Nurse, could you get me a decaffeinated coffee as well.' Mrs Froome bellowed, in her Leicester accent trying to make it sound posh.

'I'd like decaffeinated pee.' Shouted Mrs Rawlings,

'And I'd like a gin and tonic.' Miss Jones added, by this time Felicity was looking a bit bemused and I was glaring at the mischief makers. The other nurses were sniggering and even Sister was finding it difficult not to smile.

'Hurry up Nurse, my chauffeur will be here soon to take me home,' cried Mrs Smith who was being discharged that day. I could see this was going to get out of hand.

'Come on Miss Wright, let's get you back to bed.' I said. I was still trying to work out how I could fulfil the request as there were no shops nearby and Sister wouldn't let me off the ward anyway so I was greatly relieved when we got to her room and she said.

'There's a jar of decaffeinated coffee in my locker nurse.' I could still hear the laughter from the ward where the other patients were when I went to the kitchen to make the coffee although they had moved on to stories about Mrs Rawling's nephew who worked as a bouncer in a nightclub.

I needed to follow the instructions on the coffee jar as I wasn't sure if it was made in the same way as normal coffee but was relieved to find it was. I took the coffee into the side room and spent the next few days looking after Felicity as none of the others would go near her. On her last day she came onto the ward to find me and gave me a card.

'Nurse Brookes.' She said, 'I have been watching you and you will go to the very top of your profession.' With that she turned and left the ward with her head held high. For a humble second year enrolled nurse student this seemed unlikely but it was kind of her to say so. The other nurses did the rolling eyes thing again and I turned to them and said.

'What's wrong with decaffeinated coffee?' They laughed and carried on with their work.

Chapter 12

Don't Get Old Nurse

Geriatrics is now more correctly termed 'care of the elderly' but when I trained it was geriatrics and I went to the Leicester General Hospital for this placement. It was tricky getting there by bus and on a Sunday morning for an early shift I had to walk which meant leaving an hour and a half before a shift, it was torture even for a nineteen year old.

The memory of a cold Sunday morning trek across the streets of Leicester stands out clearly in my mind. I dragged myself out of bed at five thirty, having only gone to bed at midnight, quickly and quietly washed and dressed so as not to wake my mum or brother (I was living at home at the time), whispered to myself not to make a noise and slipped out of the front door, closing it as quietly as I could. It was freezing outside, there was frost on the pavements and the roads and the cold air shocked my lungs into a coughing fit. There was no-one on the streets, not even a paperboy. As I walked I began to wake up out of my sleepiness, the cold and fresh air doing their bit to bring me to an alert state. It was still quite dark when I first started out but the light forced its way through the darkness and when I walked onto the ward an hour and a half later daylight was winning and a clear winter's day was the result.

I was still coughing when I got to work, I'm sure the three cigarettes I had smoked on my way in didn't help, I hadn't given up the habit yet. There was no time to recover from the walk it was action stations as soon as I arrived, perhaps as well as canteens didn't open that early on a Sunday, in fact nothing opened that early on a Sunday apart from hospital wards.

The charge nurse was Italian, very attractive and very naughty, it was easy to see why he had become a nurse and it wasn't for the money. He had a well deserved reputation and I have to say it was very difficult not to fall for his charm, in fact I did fall for his charm and had a brief liaison with him. Brief liaisons were all he went in for as I also discovered later he was married – What is it with married men and younger models? I wasn't an angel either, I had a boyfriend. At the time of my geriatric placement I don't think I got the best professional experience as it was rather distracting falling for the man in charge. Most nurses would fall for doctors, policemen or firemen, I had to be different.

Geriatric wards were not pleasant, patients were either in bed or sat out in chairs by the bed. It made me sad to see most of these people (many of them war veterans), needing help with feeding, cutting up food, drinking and most other things. Many patients were incontinent and many were confused, either due to an acute illness or dementia. Geriatric wards were also what we called 'heavy' as we were constantly lifting people and moving them up and down beds, in and out of chairs, on and off commodes or bedpans. The ward was physically demanding as well as psychologically, it was an absolute tragedy to see so many sick old people all in one place. One thing that was very common on this ward was that almost every patient I helped would say.

'Don't get old nurse', as if I had a choice in the matter. It was said in a jovial kind of way, though often with a hint of sadness. As I have got older myself I begin to understand the meaning behind the sentence which was often said with a faraway look in the eyes.

Mr Broadley was a seventy eight year old gentleman who had been admitted to the ward following a fall and he had been recovering quite well. He was a quiet, shy man, who kept himself to himself and who had always looked uncomfortable being on a ward full of other people. He didn't give away very much at all for the whole time he was on the ward. One day, when I was on an early shift, following a late shift the night before, I was rushing around helping people eat their meals. It had been yet another heavy and busy shift and I was really looking forward to my own lunch break. I was now clearing away lunch trays. I got to Mr Broadley and found he hadn't touched his dinner and as he was a patient who could feed himself I was a bit short with him.

'Come on Mr Broadley, eat your dinner.' He looked at me and said,

'I'm not very hungry.'

'Well you need to eat to get your strength up. I'll leave you with it for a bit longer,' I have no idea why I felt slightly irritated, the poor man just didn't feel hungry, probably because he was so private we hadn't built up any real rapport or perhaps I was just feeling a bit impatient and was dog tired. I left him to it and rushed off to finish all the other trays and went for lunch.

When I came back from lunch the curtains were pulled around Mr Broadley's bed, there was a hush on the ward and I sensed immediately what had happened. He had been found dead in his chair an hour after our conversation, fork still in his hand. I felt absolutely gutted, not because he had died as many patients died and a quick death was often a blessing in disguise. I was gutted because the last words he had heard from another person on this earth consisted of a rebuke over eating his dinner and because inwardly I had felt mildly annoyed with him.

No kind last words, no compassion or empathy, just 'eat your dinner' and then this quiet man exited the world. The guilt I felt over this was immense and if I could only have turned the clock back, I would have asked him how he was feeling, whether he had any pain, squeezed his hand, anything but 'eat your dinner'. This was another reminder that nursing was no ordinary job, if I worked in an office and got irritated with someone there would usually be time to patch it up, get over it but in nursing, particularly geriatrics death was common and what I said to people mattered. Later, when his family came to see the body, I could barely look them in the eye, when the porters came to collect the body his daughter looked at me and with tears in her eyes, said,

'Please look after him, I know he's just another patient to you, but he's my dad.' As if I didn't feel bad before, I felt fifty times worse now, was she a mind reader? I assured her I would treat him with dignity and respect, which I did and when he had left the ward, I went to the toilet and cried my eyes out. I felt like I was the worst nurse in the world and it would take me quite a while to get over that one. I would like to say I have never been irritated with a patient since but I am human and have all the frailties that go with this but I do the best I can in a stressful, emotionally demanding and ever changing job.

Mrs Renshaw was a ninety year old who had been admitted via the medical ward following recovery from breathing problems related to congestive cardiac failure (now known as heart failure), she was breathless after a few yards and a little bit forgetful but other than that she was amazing. The physiotherapist tried to get her to use a walking frame but as soon as she was out of sight Mrs Renshaw would trot down the ward without any walking aids, only stopping due to breathlessness.

'Mrs Renshaw.' I protested, 'you know you are supposed to walk with the Zimmer frame. What will the Physio say?'

'She can say what she likes.' Mrs Renshaw replied with a twinkle in her eye. 'It won't fit in my house and I will be going home soon, I don't like being here with all these old people.'

'Really, you know most of them are younger than you of course?'

'Humph, I'm still the youngest here because I feel young, I looked after my mother and my aunt until they died but there's no-one to look after me so I will look after myself.' There was a bit of logic to her argument but she did look very frail and was so out of puff most of the time, I feared she might not be able to look after herself for very much longer but she did have a steely determination that kept her going.

'I was a teacher you know, nurse and I ruled my classes with a rod of iron, I think this ward is sloppy and it comes from the top.' She nodded towards the Charge Nurse, 'he needs to get a grip and tighten the reigns,' she continued.

'What do you mean?' I asked, we were both looking at him flirting with a Staff Nurse who had come to the ward to borrow equipment. I think I knew exactly what she meant.

'Look at him, he can't keep his eye off the ladies, he is so gallant but the staff' under him are too familiar with him and that leads to ill discipline, which in turn leads to shoddiness. Look under that bed nurse, dust, you wouldn't get that if he was good at his job.' With that she trotted off down the ward having totally disarmed me in relation to the Zimmer frame. I smiled to myself as I had been duped by a ninety year old. I did keep an eye out for 'shoddiness' on the ward after that but other than a few bits of dust and the wheels not all pointing in the right direction, the care was very good and the patients' who could respond seemed very happy with our rather dishy Italian especially when he flirted with them as well.

In contrast to the death and dying of geriatrics the social life at the hospital was good, there were often parties held by doctors. Doctors mess parties were regular events and all nurses were invited, surprise, surprise. 'Mess' parties were an apt term as they usually were very messy events. Doctors letting their hair down, so to speak, no different to university antics really and as most of the doctors were fresh out of university this was not surprising. There was always a lot of alcohol and lots of nurses looking for their ideal husband and lots of doctors looking for their ideal one night stand.

Some doctor-nurse relationships do end in marriage but more don't. There was the obvious pecking order in relation to doctors and nurses to complicate matters, a bit like men and women in those days too but enrolled nurses were at the bottom of this pecking order. I can't say it was something I noticed early on but it became apparent when I was doing my registered nurse training as I would hear comments about enrolled nurses then, that I had never heard as an enrolled nurse. No wonder some SENs had a chip on their shoulder. My ex boyfriend, a GP once, arrogantly referred to SENs as 'sub normally educated nurses'. I knew from that moment on we were never going to be serious. I found the comment offensive and arrogant. Anyway back to doctors parties, they were good for a laugh but I never met a doctor, other than said GP who I wanted to go out with and he confirmed why this was. Please don't get me wrong, I have met some lovely doctors who do a great job and some are friends. I should of course add the addendum that I lack the kind of commitment needed for a marriage anyway.

Chapter 13

Jonathan Livingston Seagull

My psychiatric ward placement occurred a bit later in my career when I was training for the Registered General Nurse (RGN) qualification in my early twenties. A few months prior to starting the placement I had given up smoking and was doing really well but there were a few occasions during this placement when I could easily have started again.

The hospital was on the outskirts of a village fourteen miles from the nearest town. This was often the case for old psychiatric hospitals. I had recently passed my driving test and my dad had bought me a mini. I remember taking the train up to Leicester to collect the car he had bought for me. It was a jet black Mini 'B' registration which meant it was very old. My dad proudly presented the car to me and gave me the keys. Oh dear, I had only just passed my driving test and I was going to have to drive this car from Leicester to Reading where I was now living. At least I had ridden a motorbike for a while, although never on the motorways.

I got into the car and managed to find my way to the M1, I was driving in the inside lane and got about halfway down when I noticed smoke coming from the engine. I pulled onto the hard shoulder having no idea what to do. I hadn't joined a breakdown service. Thankfully a man in a van pulled in seeing my dilemma, he opened the bonnet for me as I didn't know where the latch was for this and the smoke was pouring from the radiator.

'Radiator's dry, love.' He said. 'We'll let it cool off for a bit and then I'll tow you to the next service station.' My knight in shining armour did just this and even showed me how to fill the radiator with water. Thankfully the radiator hadn't burst but he poured in some liquid that would fix any small cracks just in case. 'You've got an oil leak as well, you'll need to get the gasket checked when you get home.' I'd had enough of foreign languages for one day but nodded anyway. My dad had bought the car for fifty pounds and I was beginning to see why.

The stories of my relationship with this car which managed to stay on the road for about a year could be the subject of a short book. Whenever I drove it, smoke would come into the car through the dashboard much to the alarm of any friends who got in.

'Don't worry, I'll open the window.' I would say, needless to say many of my friends wouldn't even get in. The passenger door wouldn't open and so any person who was brave enough to get in, had to enter through the driver's door. I was dropping a friend off after an evening event to the nursing home where she lived when I reversed into a ditch. My friend was African and was used to broken things so she took it all in her stride. We ended up calling the pastor from my church, who kindly came and towed me out of the ditch. He was surrounded by giggling student nurses, poor man. My last journey in the car occurred one day the next year. I had left a friend's flat and got two hundred yards down the road when my faithful friend gave up the ghost. My friend was delighted and said she had prayed the car off the road, I was gutted.

The car did manage to get me to and from the psychiatric hospital for my placement, although I did occasionally borrow a friend's car. The grounds of the hospital were beautiful with a long winding driveway to the main hospital building with green lawns, flower beds and an abundance of trees. A wildlife haven; I was to work on an acute psychiatric ward although there were some long stay patients on the ward as well.

Some patients on psychiatric wards are admitted compulsorily under what is commonly known as 'sectioning', a part of the Mental Health Act that allows people to be admitted against their will for their own or the public's safety. Many of these patients are manifesting psychotic behaviour and have little or no insight into their condition, usually refusing treatment and not taking medication. For a general nurse, working on a psychiatric ward can be a little bit frightening and for me it was going to be very testing from day one.

The first problem I encountered was that I found it very difficult to tell the patients from the staff. Psychiatric nurses seemed to be a completely different breed and they managed to blend in. This was made more difficult because they didn't wear uniform, this makes sense because uniforms do create a barrier and often hinder effective communication on level terms but it certainly didn't help me and of course I stuck out like a sore thumb as I had to wear uniform.

The first thing I noticed was the large sitting room with a TV and stereo, for obvious reasons this was not like a ward at all so I was in an unfamiliar environment from the outset. There was also an activities room with a large table tennis table that dominated the space. There were tables and chairs with chess and other games boards and some residents were painting. It was like smoky Joe's cafe and reminded me of a pub but not in a pleasant way. A thick smog hung in the air and my lungs would fill up with the second hand nicotine I had recently given up.

It seemed to me that every patient and every member of staff smoked, this was really not helping me – my first thoughts were that this was going to be tough. I stuck out and it was going to be really hard not to, obviously I had no clue what I was doing and I must have looked permanently bemused. That's because I was permanently bemused. There was little in the way of routine on a psychiatric ward apart from medicine rounds although these too were performed in a rather haphazard way and I was always amazed how patients got the correct medicines, if indeed they did.

There were therapy sessions and meal times. The rest of the time there was no, 'hurry up nurse,' at all, the pace was slow and sometimes dull. The idea was to communicate with patients rather than rush around carrying out tasks and whilst I agreed with the ethos it was difficult to slow myself down, having been on the treadmill of general nursing for a few years. Of course I had always spent time with patients and got to know them as much as I could within the constraints of hospital life but this was very different. I felt out of my depth.

Mrs Jacobs was one of the first people I met, an elderly lady of seventy six years, who was a long stay patient, having been in the hospital for the best part of thirty years. Mrs Jacobs was on the ward as the other long stay wards were full and she was safe enough to move. She was short and a little bit obese with deep wrinkles set in a round, pale face, on reflection I'm sure she had a curved nose, looking like a witch caricature. She looked terrifying enough but this was made worse by the fact that she always wore black which added a deathly air to her demeanour. One day I was coming on duty and she was sat out on the veranda in front of the ward in the rain. I should have known better than to try and bring sense into her world.

'Come on in from the rain Mrs Jacobs, you'll get wet out here.'

'Get lost, GOD TOLD ME TO SIT OUT HERE!' she shouted. Naively I thought a little bit of gentle persuasion would help and so I tried to gently take her arm. Next thing I knew she flew out of the chair like an eighteen year old, grabbed me by the arms and inches from my face yelled.

'GOD TOLD ME TO SIT HERE!' This time I believed

her and thanking God she hadn't thumped me I sheepishly went onto the ward to see what else awaited me that day.

The shifts in psychiatry were very long, twelve hours, I had to adapt to a different pace of life. As previously mentioned, there was no hustle and bustle that I had been used to. Much of the day was spent chatting to patients or attending therapy sessions. Some days I went home feeling I had not had one conversation that wasn't bizarre either with staff or patient. Mainly this was because I hadn't had a conversation that wasn't bizarre.

Nowadays students have mentors when on a placement so that they know who to go to if they have any questions and the mentor helps them settle into a placement. Sadly there was no such luxury during my psychiatric placement, I never knew who I would be working with from one day to the next and although the staff were nice enough, I think they felt that general nurses were just not on the same wavelength, which of course was true, I was never on the same wavelength and no-one stands out as particularly helpful. Some nurses just aren't cut out for psychiatry although I did try to make the best of it and to understand some of the conditions people presented with.

Pete was nineteen years old and suffering from manic depression, now known as bipolar disorder he would have mood swings from extremes of high to low and back again, he was apparently going through a depressive stage. Conversations therefore were monosyllabic and morose. I had been instructed by the psychiatric nurse to try to motivate him into talking about happy things. I would begin by saying something like,

'Tell me about your happy memories.' He began telling me about a happy time when his family were altogether and I thought I was doing great but very soon he was at the family arguments, the divorce, his illness and before long we were back to the lows. He was a lovely looking young lad, average height, good body, hazel eyes and long black hair. Of course he wore black which seemed to be standard attire on the ward, particularly in the depressive stages of mental illness. I got to know him quite well and it transpired he was a Christian but didn't feel that he was doing very well at this as mental illness was sometimes frowned upon. We talked about his faith a lot and this always brightened him up, often by the end of the day he was feeling much more positive but usually by the next morning we had to start over again.

I remember Pete going for electroconvulsive therapy (ECT, electric shock treatment) and coming back in a much worse state than before he went in. I was never convinced about this rather barbaric treatment in spite of being assured by the psychiatric nurses (who still seemed like many of the patients) that it worked. I got into trouble with the ward sister for refusing to accompany and observe ECT, I tried to argue that one should be able to conscientiously object to the treatment which was by no means proven and seemed like an extreme last resort which should have been reserved for the likes of William the Conqueror rather than twentieth century nursing. She wasn't having any of this and said that I was lucky I was a general nurse or I would be out on my ear. I won the battle but obviously not the war.

There was pandemonium one day when Pete went missing, staff were sent out to look for him and his parents had been informed, the psychiatric nurses were searching the village and the pubs (any excuse) but for once I felt confident that I knew this patient better than they did and as I was surplus to requirements they let me go look. I walked through the beautiful grounds that in another world would have been so peaceful and around the driveway to the hospital Chapel. There was Pete, sitting in one of the pews, head bowed, praying. I waited for him to move and then told him that the whole world was searching for him as he was not supposed to leave the ward unsupervised. I asked him how he had managed to get out as the ward was a 'lock up'.

'I just walked out with one of the visitors.' He smiled, he looked brighter and it was from here he turned the corner, his demeanour changed along with his clothing colour, at least he went into greys and blues rather than blacks. We went happily back to the ward and I thought maybe I could enjoy psychiatry after all.

Henrietta was another patient with depression who was in her mid fifties, she was average height, overweight with thick grey hair, she was a very good artist and when she was recovering, painted lovely scenic watercolours. She was nearing the time for discharge as she had made good progress in the therapy sessions and was conversing in a normal way. By that I mean her speech would vary rather than be monotone which she often demonstrated in the depressed stage of her illness. I came in one morning and she looked dishevelled, scruffy, dressed in dark brown and she showed me the paintings she had been working on. These paintings were of various unrecognisable creatures with evil eyes eating harmless animals such as pet dogs and there were lots of dark colours in them.

'That's what's inside me,' she stated and, even I, knew we were back to square one. It was very disheartening. At least with Henrietta it was clear from her paintings what was going on inside her head, it was not always as clear as this.

Therapy sessions were held each morning for a group of patients, with a psychiatrist, a psychiatric nurse and a therapist. As a student I would attend quite a few of these, as an observer of course. The sessions were aimed at getting the patients to communicate and to share their problems with each other. I apologise to modern day psychiatric nurses if you think I am ignorant, I know that patients are now called clients but they weren't at the time.

Group therapy appeared to be chaotic with either one patient dominating proceedings or everyone sitting in silence hoping that someone else would speak. The psychiatric professionals were at ease with the silence and so I felt this must be good, although I had to sit on my hands to stop myself fidgeting and of course my mind would wander. One particularly long, silent session I remember was where a patient called Gerald had muttered.

'I feel very low.' We waited to see what words of wisdom the psychiatrist was going to offer for an inordinately long time. The psychiatrist, Dr Jason looked like he was in a daze, the therapist's feet started to shuffle and other staff were also looking at him to see what he was going to say as he usually offered some leadership and guidance. After a long time, the psychiatric nurse looked at Gerald, who was looking at the floor and then at Dr Jason.

'Gerald has said he is feeling very low doctor.' Dr Jason appeared not to hear and finally said.

'Very good, same time tomorrow then,' he got up to leave, muttering on his way out. 'Oh yes, good session, see you all tomorrow,' and off he went leaving everyone staring after him in disbelief. We were all dismissed and the therapist stayed behind to speak to Gerald. We didn't see Dr Jason the next day as he was off sick with depression would you believe.

Dr Bradley led the sessions for the next few weeks and they were a lot more lively and engaging and I found I quite enjoyed them. Looking back I don't know how on earth we didn't recognise the signs of depression in Dr Jason but I think we just forgot that doctors and nurses are human too and as such, susceptible to the same illnesses and weaknesses that happen to patients. We become so good at acting and putting on the professional persona that we sometimes neglect ourselves to our own detriment. I have frequently witnessed nurses and doctors over the years needing help but finding it very difficult to acknowledge their own frailty. I think we gain the misperception that because we are in the caring profession and people look to us for help that we must always be the perfect support to everyone else to the detriment of caring for ourselves sometimes.

One day I was asked to keep an eye on Julie, a teenager with anorexia. Julie was eighteen years old and had suffered from anorexia since she was fourteen when for no obvious reason, she began to believe she was fat. Initially she had managed to hide it from her parents who felt that she was just going through a teenage phase but it became increasingly obvious that she was unwell, when she lost masses of weight and her parents would hear her vomiting in the bathroom after being encouraged to eat.

Doctors had excluded any physical cause and Julie had been just over five stone on admission to the ward under a Section as her health was deteriorating so rapidly she was at risk of starvation. She was now six stone but still very thin and wasted, looking rather like a skeleton on legs, she had light brown, curly hair and freckles and would have been very attractive at a normal weight but she still insisted she was overweight and that we were making her look obese. During therapy sessions, Julie was always quiet but one day she did say that she felt fat.

'What makes you think that?' asked Dr Bradley,
'My best friend' she said.

'Did your best friend say you were fat?' Asked the therapist,

'The girls at school called her fatty' Julie said and finally there was something to work on with Julie and the mood in the therapy session became very upbeat. It transpired that Julie's best friend was overweight and had been teased at school about this. While her best friend had found it upsetting, she had not taken it too seriously, whereas Julie had developed a fear of bullying by proxy.

On this particular day I had been told to observe her and try to make sure that after eating she didn't go and throw up anywhere. Dutifully I chatted to Julie and stayed with her most of the day. At some point, though, I must have been distracted and she gave me the slip – no point applying to CI5 then. I worked out that she would probably be in the toilets getting rid of her dinner and I was right. On entering the toilet I saw her and she was furious at being caught out, or maybe she was hungry having just thrown up her dinner, because she grabbed my hand, duly bit my wrist and then left.

I had been taken completely by surprise, boy, did it hurt, I had human teeth marks on my wrist for weeks and was lucky the wound didn't get infected. Stupidly I didn't report it and didn't get a tetanus injection but luckily I was ok. I really didn't like psychiatry. I should have reported the incident but nobody had told me this and I should have had a tetanus shot and gamma globulin shot, human bites are actually quite serious and prone to infection due to the many bacteria living in the mouth.

Nurses were prone to injuries from patients, usually though from those that were confused or demented. I gave Julie a wide berth after that incident and was always on my guard if she came anywhere near me, she was a smiling tiger I decided.

Emily was in her early thirties, a lady with schizophrenia who was put in a room with Mrs Jacobs. They seemed to get on very well together as they could have rather strange conversations among themselves without either of them getting upset because they didn't listen to each other. Emily was very pretty with long dark brown hair and big blue eyes. She had been a bit of a loner as a child and tended to move between jobs. On returning to her home from one of these she became very suspicious of her family and she felt they were plotting against her and that she was in danger. She eventually changed the wiring in various plugs around the house, stopped eating and barricaded herself into her room becoming aggressive towards her family. She was admitted to the ward under Section 25 of the Mental Health Act of the time. When I first met her she seemed bewildered and would giggle inappropriately, she was convinced that creatures were coming out of her food and her skin. Once she had seemingly settled in I went and sat with her, she looked frightened and her eyes kept darting about as if she was seeing something or someone that I couldn't see. Eventually she said.

'What do you want to know?'

'My name is Dawn, what's yours?' Is all I could

think of to say.

She smiled and giggled. 'I'm a dancer, just come back from Thailand.' This was good I thought, she is at least having a conversation, 'they were all evil, I used to dance out of time to the music.'

'Why did you do that?'

'Because they were evil, they are evil in here too.' And so the conversation continued, she would jump from one subject to another making me think I had missed something but it was her thoughts that were all jumbled up coming out in spates intermingled with long silences, where she would stare into space as if to go somewhere else. I thought how awful it must be for her, suspicious of everybody. Most of the time Emily appeared emotionless but sometimes she would display anger at being in hospital against her will and said she wanted to go home. Much of the time she would be accusing people of trying to poison her and she became quite frightened.

One evening she tried to run away, walking off the ward in the middle of a conversation, I caught up with her and asked her to come back. She refused and a male nurse came to offer support, what followed was a scuffle and the male nurse and another nurse escorted her firmly back to the ward. I felt ill, I had never had to physically force anyone to stay on a ward against their will and it didn't sit at all comfortably with me, except, perhaps in the case of Phil.

Phil, a man recently admitted was tall and slim with lovely blond hair and sky blue eyes, he was seventeen and thought he was Jonathan Livingston Seagull. Jonathan Livingstone Seagull is a story about a seagull who, realises that there is more to life than being with ordinary seagulls so he is transported to a much higher plane and he is sent back to tell other seagulls about it, this causes a seagull rebellion with many young seagulls following after Jonathan. Phil was trying to get people to follow him to this plane.

Phil had become psychotic from LSD drug use and he was definitely in another world. He felt that he should be allowed to fly free, he had indeed tried to fly off a roof once but broke an ankle rather than escaping to another world, he wanted to get away from the ordinary seagulls (us) and we were hindering his freedom. Sometimes his world was nice and sometimes terrifying. He could instantly change from laughing and joking one minute to throwing furniture and anything he could get his hands on the next as I discovered one day when I came on shift.

Phil was sitting in a chair in the lounge and suddenly, for no apparent reason, he stood up marched across the room, picked up an armchair and threw it across the room, fortunately it didn't hit anyone. Bedlam then ensued, he jumped through a window and threw missiles at everyone passing, Staff' were ducking missiles while trying to isolate Phil and move other patients to safety. The whole ward became carnage in a matter of minutes, he was winding up all of the very vulnerable patients and it was becoming more chaotic by the minute. It was actually one of the most frightening experiences I ever had as a nurse, I was scared of him, I have to admit, he was uncontrollable, imagine someone like this out in public.

After about forty five minutes when he had run out of missiles, staff had finally managed to corner him and he was then removed forcibly, locked in a room with nothing but a mattress on the floor and given a sedative injection to calm him, funnily enough I had no problem with this. I was just relieved that no-one was seriously injured, although Phil had managed to cut himself with glass from the window and one member of staff had sustained a cut lip from a missile.

Psychiatric nurses went up in my estimation that day, they somehow managed to maintain an element of calm, (calm being relative here), protect other patients and handle Phil, firmly but without any anger or too much evidence of stress although there obviously was a little. Sometimes, with Phil on the ward it reminded me of the film *One Flew over the Cuckoo's Nest.*

After the event with Phil, I realised that Emily had also been detained by force because she was in hospital under a Section and there was a duty of care to keep her there until the Section ran out. Eventually she responded to medication and became less suspicious. When her Section ran out the review panel decided she could no longer be kept in under a Section but she was advised to stay in as a voluntary patient. On my last day on the ward, oh happy day.... I went to say goodbye to

Emily who was due to go home the following week.

'I just want to tell you a secret, come here.' She said in a conspiratorial fashion. I felt honoured and I leaned over to her so she could whisper in my ear.

'I have been in Mrs Jacob's body,' she said and then giggled. Still some work to be done then, I thought and was glad to leave psychiatric wards behind me. Definitely not cut out to be a psychiatric nurse was my conclusion. Thankfully some nurses are.

I recently met someone who reminded me of Emily, a woman in her late sixties who had married the patient I was visiting. When I arrived I asked what the problem was with their letter box as I had noticed it was all taped up from the inside.

'The neighbours are putting poisonous gas through the letter box.' Mrs Buxton replied. On asking if she had any other problems with the neighbours she explained that they were coming through the walls at night, they had recently arrived and had been following her from house to house as she kept moving to try to escape from them. She tried to point out some of the neighbours standing at the bottom of her garden. I looked but couldn't see anyone. The frightening thing was that her husband, who she had recently married, was also beginning to enter her world.

Over time I managed to gain her consent for a psychiatric referral but the psychiatric nurse only managed one visit before she upped sticks again and moved away from the people who were after her. I had never been able to contact her children as she wouldn't let me have their information. A note had gone into her medical records this time, so that the next GP would be alerted when she registered with a surgery and hopefully help would be available.

Chapter 14

'Treadmill Nurse'

Surgical wards were very different to medical wards in that the turnover was faster and there was more of a mixed age group. Surgeons, I discovered, were a different breed of doctor to others, skilful when it came to operating but bedside manner, often sadly lacking. They would arrive on a ward surrounded by an entourage of white coats, look for Sister, who wasn't hard to find to be fair as she would be on high 'ward round' alert. The surgeon would then begin the ward round. I am not sure if they are all sporty but they walk and talk at a rate of knots that others find difficult to follow.

Many surgeons absolutely love showing off, the poor senior house officer (all but junior doctor) would explain what the patient had been admitted with for example, pain in the groin and then tell the surgeon what they have done so far. A nice surgeon would coax a diagnosis out of the SHO but the Mr Barnes and many others like him, would snap questions, belittle the answers and then reassure the patient that he would be the one looking after them as he was surrounded by imbeciles, he would then conclude by muttering something under his breath like:

'Let's remove half the bowel. That should do the trick.' The SHO would go bright red, the medical students would smirk and appreciate it wasn't them being belittled for a change and the poor patient would stare after the entourage, already half way down the ward surrounding the next person. Ok so this might be slightly exaggerated (poetic license) but the gist is true. Brilliance often comes with caveats.

One thing about hospital wards that has always been a mystery to me is the curtains surrounding beds. Obviously they serve a purpose in relation to visual privacy, although on a surgical ward round the sister was lucky if she managed to get them closed before the entourage were moving to the next bed. I think sometimes consultants deliberately waited for the curtains to be closed before they marched through them leaving someone, usually a nurse trying to open them and then quickly close the next lot before the doctors moved on again. It was actually quite funny.

As I said before, the curtains do offer some visual privacy so that the patient can be examined by the doctor and all the medical students can take their turn examining – if the patient didn't have much pain prior to the round they would certainly have enough after five pairs of hands had prodded them thoroughly. In terms of confidentiality though, curtains offer no protection whatsoever, every patient would know what was happening to the patient next to them by the end of the round which was perhaps as well as they could then interpret what had been said to them. Seriously there are some major issues around confidentiality on hospital wards, in fact, now with the six bed bays it is much worse, as at least on a forty bed Nightingale ward, the high ceilings helped dissipate some noise and space in between the beds was larger.

For nurses on surgical wards there were admission and discharge procedures with everything in between.

'Hurry up nurse take this tube out; hurry up nurse I need a bedpan; hurry up nurse this patient needs to go to theatre, x ray, Timbuktu and so on.' We were often left trying to explain to the patient what the surgeon had said, that's if we had managed to pick up what they had said, junior doctors' might try but their knowledge was as limited if not more so than ours. Thankfully Sister would do a daily round of patients herself and explain everything.

There was always some procedure going on, during the ward round the surgeon would often say.

'Take it out nurse.' Referring to the removal of stitches; clips; wound drains; catheters; drips (intravenous infusions); naso-gastric tubes, to mention just a few. In addition to this we had to check drips, dress wounds, put in catheters, naso-gastric tubes, remove said tubes, put up parenteral nutrition which was then in its infancy and much more besides.

In preparing a person for theatre they had to have a bath, remain nil by mouth for an inordinately unnecessary length of time and then have the area shaved that was to be operated on and finally put on an operating gown. In the 1970's men would shave men's genital areas and women, women, if a male nurse was not available the doctor would do the male shave, otherwise Sister would do it. Female nurses were not allowed to catheterise men nor men women, although male and female doctors could do both. This practice has changed now and female nurses carry out all of the tasks to both male and females and vice versa for male nurses although female patients occasionally refuse male nurses.

Once ready for theatre the patient was accompanied by a nurse to the anaesthetic room until they had been given the anaesthetic. It was rewarding in many ways, people would usually be admitted in pain and eventually leave the ward happy – assuming the right part had been removed that is. I have fortunately not been involved in a situation where the wrong kidney or leg has been removed but I have read the newspapers like everyone else.

During training I had to undertake four practical assessments that had to be passed prior to finals, these included:

- A medical assessment – bed bath
- A sterile procedure assessment – any dressing or procedure requiring use of an aseptic technique
- A medicines round assessment – a full medicines round
- A management assessment – managing the ward for a shift

The dreaded assessment day had arrived, this

one was a sterile procedure assessment and Sister Rowntree was coming from the School of Nursing to assess me. I had chosen to do a suture removal for this and had asked one of the patients, Mrs Flowers permission to do this for my assessment and explained the Tutor would be there to make sure I did it properly.

'That's fine *me* duck,' she had said in full Leicester twang.

I had arrived onto shift early to prepare myself and remind Mrs Flowers.

'Don't worry, you'll pass,' she had tried to reassure me. I kept looking around for Sister Rowntree who was due any minute, the inevitable butterflies were in my stomach, I had met with Sue before going on shift, she had passed her assessment the week before, Bette was doing hers the following week and Charlie & Grace had passed theirs in their previous placement. This was my second assessment as the first had been a bed bath in my first year. Sister was leaving me alone today, knowing I would be nervous and therefore useless until the assessment was out of the way, she had given me a light workload. Finally, the footsteps were heard above all the din of the ward, the unmistakeable clop, clop of high heels on marble. Clinical tutors and Night Sisters were the only staff who got away with wearing heels in hospital. I think Night Sisters wore them deliberately so that they wouldn't catch us doing anything we shouldn't be! I went to meet her.

'Good afternoon Nurse Brookes,' Sister

Rowntree said, no smile, the tutors rarely smiled before or during an assessment even if they were nice.

'Good afternoon Sister,' I replied.

'Let's get on with it then, who are we seeing today?'

'Mrs Flowers, a sixty year old lady who had a laparotomy and division of adhesions ten days ago Sister, her stitches are due out today and she has given consent for me to remove them.' Strictly speaking, patients were not supposed to be prepped prior to an assessment but we all did it, choosing a patient who was unlikely to cause us any additional trauma to that of being watched.

I walked towards the treatment room with Sister in tow, here I had to wash my hands correctly before setting up the dressing trolley. I cleaned the trolley with a sterile antiseptic wipe starting at the top, making sure I cleaned the legs and then the bottom shelf before ending at the bottom just to the wheels. I then had to wash my hands again before placing the equipment on the trolley. I placed a dressing pack unopened along with the extras I would need on the bottom shelf, these included, cetrimide, an antiseptic for cleaning the wound (no longer used) and a stitch cutter. Once ready I pushed the trolley towards the patient, making sure I only touched the legs below the top shelf. Katy joined us at this point, another second year who was to be my 'dirty nurse'. I could feel my hands shaking already, this was going to be a long procedure. Mrs Flowers was beaming as we arrived at the bedside, the patients were always very helpful when we were doing an assessment and did their best to make sure we passed, I'm sure they would have smiled even if we totally botched it which of course some did.

'Good afternoon Mrs Flowers, I am Nurse Brookes, this is Sister Rowntree who will be observing me today and this is Nurse Jackson. We are going to take your stitches out today is that alright?' Thankfully, during the prep I had explained that I would have to introduce myself, in spite of the patient knowing who I was otherwise she would have looked at me as if I was the one who should be in the bed!

'Hello Nurses, hello Sister,' she beamed, 'Thank you Nurse, I'm sure you'll be as gentle as you always are.' She continued with a wink. Sister smiled slightly, knowing exactly what the patient was up to but pleased nevertheless. The Clinical Tutors could immediately tell if we had a good rapport with patients and would be very worried if this wasn't present.

'I'm just going to pull the curtains and then Nurse Jenkins and I will go and wash our hands.' Once back from hand washing, Nurse Jenkins took the dressing pack and peeled it open allowing the sterile pack to drop on the top shelf of the trolley without any of the unsterile bits touching it, this was an art in itself, too close and the outer packaging would touch and too far and the sterile pack could end up anywhere. After this she explained to Mrs Flowers that she would need to fold back the covers and expose the abdomen while keeping her top covered by nightdress and bottom half covered by bedding.

Meanwhile I carefully took the corners of the dressing pack and peeled it open, the first thing I had to do was attach a paper bag to the side of the trolley for the waste, I then had to take the sterile cover from the top and place it below the wound without touching the patient in the process as we didn't wear gloves for these procedures. I then took up the forceps, one in each hand and carefully set out the contents of the dressing pack neatly. After I had the gallipot (small stainless steel dish) exposed, I asked Nurse Jenkins to pour in the cetrimide. Again, with care, she peeled open the plastic sachet and poured the contents into the pot. She then peeled open the cover for the suture remover and dropped it onto my sterile field.

The suture remover had a curved blade. Nurse Jenkins now removed the dressing already in place covering the wound and placed it in the bag and she was now considered unclean so if I needed any extras she would have to go and wash her hands again. This whole process took only a few minutes as we were so used to it. Sister was watching intently for any slip ups but thankfully none so far. I took a look at the wound to make sure it had healed and that the stitches were indeed ready to come out. I then had to count them out loud, I already knew from the records that there were twenty one stitches called catgut, but had to be sure. The most common skin sutures were black catgut, these are rarely used now and scars are much neater as a result.

'Right Mrs Flowers, I am just going to give the wound a clean and then I will remove the stitches.' I said.

'Go ahead Nurse,' even she was looking nervous now. After cleaning the wound I placed a piece of sterile gauze on the sterile sheet below the wound using forceps in my left hand so that I could place the stitches in and count they had all been removed at the end of the procedure, I then took the stitch cutter in my right hand. My hands were trembling a little, I took hold of one of the loose ends of the first stitch with the forceps and then slipped the blade underneath, cutting close to the skin to ensure none of the stitch that had been exposed would pass through the inside of the patient when it was removed. Thankfully the first one came out with ease and didn't stick, there was always a bit of a pull as the forceps pulled the stitch taut for cutting but Mrs Flowers was pretending not to notice.

'Didn't feel a thing Nurse,' she smiled. I smiled back and with trembling hands removed the other twenty stitches and counted out loud before discarding them in the bag. I removed alternate stitches to start with and then once sure the wound was not looking like it would open up anywhere, I removed the rest. Only two had been stuck and needed a little more pulling, at that point I could feel the sweat starting to build up and my face flushing but once they were out, I felt I could breathe again.

'There we are, Mrs Flowers, all done.' I said as I

folded away the remnants and put everything in the rubbish bag apart from the gallipot and the forceps, these would be sent for sterilising.

'Thank you Nurse, what a great Nurse you are,' she smiled at Sister who smiled back. My job wasn't quite finished, we had to return to the treatment room, dispose of the waste and clean the trolley, finally washing my hands I turned to Sister. She smiled at last.

'Well done Nurse Brookes, you passed,' she filled out some paperwork and then left the ward and the first thing I had to do was to go and let Mrs Flowers know, you would think she had passed, she was so overjoyed. Nursing really could be a great job at times. I floated through the rest of that shift.

Sometimes because the wards were always so busy, it was easy to forget the person underneath the hospital gown, turnover was high and sometimes a reality check was required. One night I had been on a busy late shift and it was almost time for me to go home when I noticed Diana, a sixteen year old girl on a trolley with porters either end about to be whisked off to theatre with the night shift student nurse, Geraldine, looking through her list of 'to do's' for the night had not noticed that Diana was trembling. I was dead on my feet and longing to go home but I just couldn't walk away. I knew exactly how Geraldine was feeling, needing to know what she had to do before midnight was a must and there was no way she was going to notice Diana.

'Hey, Gerr,' I'll take Diana to theatre if you like, it's near the changing rooms,'

'Would you? Oh thanks Dawn, I owe you one.'
I took Diana's hand.

'Are you nervous?' She nodded and fought back tears, 'hey, don't worry, I'll be with you, nothing bad's going to happen, you'll have a lovely sleep and then the worst of this pain will go away, just a bit of a sore scar afterwards and the anaesthetist is really good looking.' She managed to smile and off we went, I held her hand and spoke to her all the way and she wouldn't let go until she was fast asleep.

'Thanks,' she said as she drifted off, and that was a reminder of what the job was all about, helping people at their most vulnerable times when all the guards are down. What a privilege and an honour it was to be a nurse I thought and somehow I was re-invigorated.

It was on a surgical ward that I first heard terms such as 'the appendix' in bed eight, 'the gall bladder in bed twelve and so on. To this day I still hear some nurses and doctors refer to patients as, 'the leg ulcers', 'the ulcerative colitis' rather than the more long winded version, Mr so and so with the leg ulcers or Mrs Jenkins who has ulcerative colitis. I know time is precious and we don't want to go all round the houses to get to the point but I think this is going a bit too far – how would a doctor like to be called, 'the moustache' or a nurse, 'the forty inch breast' (wish that were me), or even worse, 'the nose', I don't think so. Of course I was often called 'the student' so I have some understanding of how demeaning some of these terms can sound and every student reading this book will understand that one, so try not to repeat the error. I must admit we did sometimes nickname certain doctors and nurses. There was 'the beast', 'the crab', 'the voice' and so on.

The ward did have its share of sadness when a patient would come back from theatre having been opened up only for the surgeon to find that a cancer was inoperable and so would close up without removing anything.

Mr Trainer was one such patient on the receiving end of this and tried to put on such a brave face when his family visited but cried when they left. He was the first person I ever discussed dying with, he would ask questions and realise that there were no answers but it helped him to speak about how he felt. He decided not to tell his children as he didn't want them 'fussing' about him and he and his wife kept his cancer a secret for many months before he became so ill he had to tell them and he was finally admitted to hospital for one last time, his wife later told me, he died with family around his bed with as much dignity as he could muster but he was in a lot of pain.

In the late 1970's it was common practice for the relative to be told the diagnosis of cancer before the patient and they would often decide to hide it from the patient. This created incredible strain on relationships and a terrible moral dilemma for those of us involved in caring for patients. Cancer is discussed much more openly now and although it causes much distress to families at least they get the opportunity to face the disease together and even when it is incurable they get the chance to put things in order while receiving the emotional support they need from specialists such as Macmillan nurses, district nurses and palliative care consultants. Some patients though, even now, do not want to be told but are often told anyway and I have seen people go to pieces with this news and die within surprisingly short spaces of time, contrary to that which their condition would normally dictate. It never fails to amaze me the power of the human mind.

I came across many women who had to have breast or breasts removed (mastectomy), which was and probably still is, a minefield and a learning curve in the art of communication. Some women didn't seem to mind at all and were glad to have the offending article removed and some would even joke about being lopsided.

Others were distraught more about losing a breast and in some cases two, than about the diagnosis of cancer. Surgeons were perhaps a little too hasty in deciding on a mastectomy at times and with their communication skills being a little suspect, some of them added to the woman's traumatic experience. The altered body image and sense of loss that some women would go through was awful with many feeling that they could no longer be a woman.

The reaction to a mastectomy didn't seem to bear any relation to age or background and so one couldn't identify which women were going to take it badly. When it came time to remove the dressing post operatively, the clues would begin. This was usually the first opportunity for a woman to see herself without a breast and many of them found this too much to bear. We were taught not to push women to look, but to offer them the opportunity and gauge their reaction. It was never going to be easy, firstly they had to look at a great big wound with loads of stitches and often a wound drain poking out and then they had to imagine that gap without the wound. As I say, some found it easier to deal with than others. Some of the reactions would also depend on husband or partner and many men found it as difficult as the women.

Breasts have become so symbolic of womanhood and sexuality that many would find it too much. Men would often try to reassure their women but would also refuse to look at the wound area which obviously didn't inspire confidence and in many ways the psychological impact affected both partners. Men would feel guilty that they were feeling a sense of loss when the alternative (cancer and death) was so much worse and they would try to hide their feelings. Some women felt their sex life would suffer and some didn't care while some men felt the same way. As nurses we would do the best we could with the time we had, allowing each woman to decide in her own time when it was right for her to look and help to prepare them. The vast majority found that their imagination was worse than the reality and that it was not nearly as bad as they had envisaged but a very few found the opposite.

The latter would need referrals for counselling and psychiatry to assist with the adjustment. In the late 1970's and early 1980's breast implants weren't widely available and a padded bra or a false external breast was the best that could be bought, mostly not on the NHS.

Miss Henshaw, a forty nine year old lawyer, had noticed a lump in her breast while bathing and had at first ignored it hoping it would go away. After a week or two when it didn't go away she said she became obsessional about it, checking all the time to see if it was growing, hoping she was imagining it. Finally, she told her sister who insisted she go to the doctors, by this time she was imagining the worst, but hoping the doctor would tell her she was fine. The GP said he would need to refer her to the hospital to be checked out, this was before routine mammograms although she would have been too young anyway and as there was no family history of breast cancer she would not have been eligible for early mammography.

It was also before 'the two week wait' rule that now applies to suspected cancer to aid faster diagnosis in the UK. Her worst fears were confirmed twelve weeks after she had first noticed the lump, she was told she had breast cancer. I met her on the day of her admission when she was due to go to surgery the next morning for a mastectomy. Miss Henshaw was very personable and open now about the dreaded cancer, as I was taking her history she suddenly blurted out rather ironically.

'I have just finished paying the mortgage. I paid

extra because I wanted to be debt free.' I immediately understood where she was coming from – she was asking the time old question that I have noticed, people often ask when the rat race stops momentarily and they are faced with the reality of mortality.

'What is the point of it all?' Jenny was an intelligent woman and breast cancer survival rates in the early 1980's were poor although chemotherapy and radiotherapy added to the treatment options post surgery as often the cancer had spread by the time of diagnosis. Miss Henshaw came through surgery ok and she coped very well with the loss of her breast. The surgeon was optimistic that he had got the majority of the cancer and only time would tell. I admired her enormously for the dignity and bravery that she showed for the whole time she was on the ward. She would chat to other patients and help some of the older ones with their drinks and pass them things that were out of their reach while all the time she was coming to terms with the dreaded diagnosis, the loss of a breast and the fact that the next few years for her would be a walking time bomb. Her faith in God helped her in many ways, she was openly religious with a Bible on her bedside table and although she acknowledged her fears she managed to portray a sense of peace and calm.

I never saw her again after she left the ward and I don't know whether she lived a short or a long life but I don't think I have ever met anybody so ready to meet their maker as Jenny.

There was a television series filmed between 1975 and 1983 called 'Angels' I used to watch this and I loved the title (obviously) but sometimes I was certainly no angel. One Saturday morning I came on shift feeling really tired, it was a boiling hot day and the ward was heaving. I was fed up with the shifts, trying to have a social life and the constant demands of the job, it was taking its toll on me. I was a bit down in the dumps and wishing I was doing some other job in some other place and feeling very sorry for myself. Every day brought up some new tragedy for some unsuspecting person or family.

The ward was as busy as ever and I managed to put on my 'nurse' mask and as cheerfully as I could I started my tasks. I was never a person to bring problems into work, not that I really had any except that I wanted to be away from work for a while, sleep for twenty four hours and soak my tired, aching feet for as long as possible. Everything for me was a struggle that day, I felt a bit irrational, suddenly I resented the fact that I couldn't grow my finger nails, couldn't wear jewellery or nail varnish, my feet were enclosed in ugly, flat, leather shoes and I couldn't go into town with my friends and my boyfriend was going to a barbecue that afternoon without me (again he had moaned that morning). I was twenty years old but that day I felt so much older in spite of patients always saying.

'You don't look old enough to be a nurse'. Well I felt old enough, this day was going to be a struggle, maybe I should have thrown a 'sicky' but then I wouldn't have been able to go out anyway. No, there was nothing to it but to get on with it.

The morning went fairly smoothly, Sister Blunkett was in a good mood although we were short staffed as two people had gone off sick (I wondered if they had felt like me), we managed to get on with the jobs without too much interruption. One of the nice things about weekends was that there was no routine surgery and most of the patients were recovering post operatively. We had been on call the night before so the majority of emergency operations had been carried out during the night and as the ward was now full, we couldn't take any more new patients.

If I thought I was tired, I was spritely in comparison to David, the SHO who had obviously been up for most of the night, the difference was that he believed it was his right to be grumpy and punish everyone for the fact that he hadn't been to bed. In fairness to him, it wasn't unusual for a junior doctor to work for seventy two hours or more with little or no sleep, being called out in the night to prescribe medicines, re-site drips, assist in theatre, clerk in new patients to mention just a few of his jobs. Many of these things can be done by nurses now and the length of time for doctors on call was changed in 2000 as it was dangerous for patients to be looked after by doctors who had been on the go for so long. European working time directives have also changed length of junior doctors hours from fifty six to forty eight per week so if they are still moaning they need to speak to their colleagues who were often dead on their feet.

By the end of the morning I was feeling more like my normal self and having gone around the ward cheering up the patients I had managed to cheer myself up too. David had been encouraged by Sister to go and get some sleep, stating he should also have a wash and shave before he came back to the ward and he had sheepishly agreed. By the time I came back from lunch I loved my job again and floated through the afternoon bantering with patients and other nurses (perhaps I'm becoming a manic depressive I thought) but I think really I was cheered a little by noticing that the weather had taken a turn for the worse and a barbecue in the rain didn't seem that big an attraction after all, I even smiled at the thought of Jerry eating soggy burgers, not very angelic, I know.

James was one of the few male nurses I met while working on a surgical ward, he was a third year student nurse and had a great sense of humour, we became good friends. He was a bit of a ladies' man and went out with quite a few nurses during his training. I was never totally sure what the girls saw in him as he had acne and nystagmus, his eyes would flicker in different directions and it was hard not to stare. In his spare time he worked as a DJ and unlike me, he was very good at it and I expect it helped keep him out of debt and helped him afford to wine and dine his numerous girlfriends. I think we did almost become romantic once but both realised in time that we really didn't like each other in that way and so friendship was a much better option.

Our friendship fizzled out after a holiday in Yugoslavia when I got to know him better. One of my best friends at the time was a Great Ormond Street student nurse called Brenda, GOS nurses, as we called them, did a combined children and adult training course and she did her adult training in Leicester. We later met up and shared a flat when I moved to London to do cardio-thoracic training. I had become good friends with a physicist called Robert who worked at the same hospital as me and the four of us decided to take a holiday in Yugoslavia long before the war that split the country. Robert and James would be sharing a room and Brenda and I would be in another. It was a beautiful part of Yugoslavia called Rovinj, on the Adriatic coast and opposite Venice. We were excited as there was much to see and do, except that when Brenda and I got up on the first morning James was at the bar and there he stayed for the rest of the holiday. He thought we were incredibly boring because we didn't want to drink all day and we thought him ridiculous because he did and so we spent most of the holiday away from him.

The weather was gorgeous, it was the first time I had come across nude sunbathing. It was very entertaining watching men playing badminton on the beach in the nude and very difficult to keep one's eyes on the shuttlecock. Robert was good fun and joined in with most of what we wanted to do. We hired a speedboat and Robert loved frightening us with the speed. We also took the ferry over to

Venice for the day, James joined us for that and managed to stay relatively sober for the day. Don't get me wrong, we did do our fair share of drinking too but not all day, every day.

It was one of those holidays where you realise who you are compatible with and who you are not and when we got home at the end of the holiday James and I parted ways, we kept in touch for a little while but never saw each other again, an inevitable conclusion. I was by now living in London anyway and lost touch with lots of people I had met during my training in Leicester. Some people are friends for life and some are friends for a season it would seem.

Surgical wards were great fun at Christmas time as many of the beds would be empty and to cheer up the poor remaining patients who were having to spend the festive season in hospital and ourselves, who were having to work we would get one of the doctors to dress up as a patient and strap drips and drains to the willing participant then wait to see how long it took before Sister noticed. Brian, the SHO had agreed to be a patient and was lying in bed under the sheets pretending to be writhing in agony. Sister Blunkett was just about to pull the sheets back and find out what was happening when his emergency bleep went off, Brian leapt out of bed, unstrapped himself and went tearing down the ward much to the surprise and consternation of Sister who gaped after him trying to work out what had just happened. The rest of us were doubled up with laughter as were the rest of the patients on the ward. Brian reappeared on the ward later and smiled at Sister, apologising for his undignified exit, she smiled in return and explained she had left the bed for him to clean which brought him back down to earth.

One event that occurred on a surgical ward would stand out with me forever. We were told that a teenage girl was being admitted with a vaginal prolapse which in itself was unusual. I was on duty with the junior ward sister, Sister Davies, who was a bit like Penelope Keith in mannerism, she was always immaculate and was the only sister I had worked with who had long finger nails, polish and always wore makeup. Sister Davies never did a stroke of work, even paperwork was beneath her and she always had a mirror to hand in case her lipstick needed touching up. We were her minions and we knew our place. The paramedics arrived on the ward, explained that the girl had a vaginal prolapse and that they had applied a support truss like bandage and given her pethidine for pain, I went with the reluctant Sister to admit her to the ward. Sister Davies removed the bedclothes and went up in my estimation enormously, it was bedlam,

'THIS GIRL IS HAVING A BABY!' she yelled, glaring at the paramedics, while ringing the emergency bell. I have to say she was the only calm person in the whole of the ensuing chaos. 'Go and get me some syntometrine from the paediatric ward' she called to me, by that time other people were arriving and Sister Davies was in full control. You get a dressing pack and some gloves and you bleep the paediatrician.' She instructed the paramedics. I had always been taught to walk swiftly in an emergency, never run but that went right out of the window as I ran to the paediatric ward rehearsing the name of the drug I had never heard of all the way. Finally I arrived and asked urgently for the syntometrine. I had no idea what it was until later I learned that it is given in the third stage of labour to help the uterus contract and reduce the risk of post partum haemorrhage.

When I got back to the ward the baby had been rushed to the special care baby unit at a different hospital and sister was with the girl who was very upset. The outcome unfortunately was tragic, the baby died within a few hours. The poor young girl denied concealing the pregnancy saying that she had periods throughout and just thought she was gaining weight, her parents were obviously devastated. I think the paramedics were in the doghouse. They felt they had asked the right questions regarding pregnancy although in retrospect they would probably realise that vaginal prolapse in a teenager is almost unheard of whereas pregnancy is much more common. The heroine of the day was, of course, Sister Davies, who later said to me.

'Every nurse should know how to deliver a baby,' she had been a midwife in a previous life. No surprise then that a few years later I did my midwifery training. I also learned a humbling lesson from one of the patients when I was working on that surgical ward. It was yet again, one of those days where everyone was rushed off their feet, there didn't seem to be any let up and I was tired. Some days we worked so hard, rushing from here to there and back again, I would feel like I had run a marathon and sometimes my legs cried out for rest, this was one of those days. Mr Graham called for a commode which I duly took to him as he was just post surgery. I went to collect the commode and tried to dash off.

'Could I have a bowl of water?' He said, I must have looked confused because he then stated rather sharply, 'I am sure nurse, that when you have used the toilet, you wash your hands afterwards.' I was ashamed of myself and apologised, taking him a bowl of water after I had disposed of the commode. I never again forgot to give a patient the opportunity to wash their hands after using a commode, bedpan or urinal. Thank you Mr Graham.

Chapter 15

All Things Great & Small

Children's wards were a bit frightening for general nurses, everything was so different. Apart from the obvious fact that they were so much smaller and there were little things called babies, the routines were different. Most hospital wards have similar routines which take some getting used to at first but once mastered they are all very similar. Arrive on shift, have handover, get on with it: make beds, help patients wash, dress, shave (men obviously), sit out, go back to bed, bum rounds, dressing rounds, drip rounds, drinks rounds, catheter rounds, rounds, rounds, rounds....... but on paediatrics this was not the case, a bit like psychiatry but nothing like psychiatry, no rounds, relaxed atmosphere, play with kids? Ok so there were feeding rounds, trying to bottle feed sick babies could take up to an hour and there were nappy changes but babies went at different times so they couldn't be confined to 'nappy rounds'. They did have drips of course but they went through drip machines that alarmed when empty so didn't need quite as much observation.

Aprons were an absolute necessity especially as you remember we wore white uniforms – one bit of baby sick and we would have been changing all day long. Although, unfortunately babies didn't always remember to puke on the apron, shoulders were not covered and so gowns also came in handy. If a baby had pyloric stenosis there was no protection as the projectile vomiting could catch you on the other side of the room.

Diarrhoea in babies was a common problem and nappy changing posed real challenges for the novice, no sooner had the bottom been washed than more produce would be evacuated and I would have to start over. This procedure could take ages and the staff nurses would laugh when they saw my face scrunched up in concentration while the baby would be screaming its head off. I began to feel an empathy with every mother on the planet. Until I did midwifery though, all babies looked alike to me and while I could coo, coo with the best of them they were not my cup of tea, far too much wailing and pooing for my liking, but the poor little ones were ill and couldn't exactly let us know how they felt in measured tones.

The paediatric wards were a mixture of medical and surgical at the time, there were cubicles for children and babies with infectious disease such as diarrhoea and vomiting and these children were barrier nursed. Each cubicle had a trolley outside with fresh gowns, masks and gloves, hands were washed before donning oneself in the garb. I often tried to imagine myself as a baby or very young child in a strange cot in a cubicle looking for mummy and in comes an apparition of light blue, with the only visible thing being the eyes. Bearing in mind people have all sorts of eyes and they are the window to the soul, no wonder there was a lot of crying from the cubicles. Babies sometimes just want to be cuddled but nurses didn't really have the time to go through the rigmarole of all that washing and changing to give a baby a cuddle so it was always a great relief when parents were around.

Some parents, like some nurses were better than others at their job and there were many times when I reluctantly handed a baby over to what I may have considered to be a bad parent. There has always been a fine line between bad parenting and abuse (the latter would be dealt with by more senior staff) but I just wished some parents would leave off child bearing.

The ward sisters and qualified staff on children's wards were, without exception wonderful human beings. There must be a reason why one becomes a paediatric nurse or a psychiatric nurse. I must apologise to all my psychiatric nursing colleagues, I love you all really. Anyway children's wards were happy places once you got used to not being watched and not being told off for talking to patients. I was still young although I felt a lot older and so I could still remember how to play. We were even allowed to call each other by our first names and the children were able to too.

Medicines were an absolute mystery, injections were usually given in micrograms rather than milligrams and at 0.1ml and other such oddities. Other medicines were given in liquid form and the calculations were complicated until we got the hang of it. Fortunately we were well supervised and the calculations did get easier with time. In recent years nurses have had trouble even calculating adult dosages since simple maths appears to be beyond many. A maths entrance exam has now been introduced to ensure nurses can tell the difference between 250mg and 125mg and between 0.3ml and 1ml, I am oversimplifying the situation but I am sure you get the meaning.

Sister Chang was a lovely ward sister, who I worked with on a paediatric ward. I was near the end of my training and on night duty on Christmas Eve. Her parting words after handover were.

'Remember, we are not on call so do not accept any new admissions.' It was a quiet night and so we decided to fill all the cubicles with dolls and put up drips and various other bits of equipment just to complicate things. We also filled some of the beds on the ward which Sister wouldn't examine closely first thing in the morning. I remember the doors being flung open in the morning as she walked past all the cubicles with trolleys outside, she came storming onto the ward.

'I thought I said no admissions!' Her voice had become very high pitched.

'I'm really sorry Sister, the other paediatric ward was full and the Nursing Officer said we had to accept all the extras, there's a bug going round.' I lied. Anyway we sat down and she did look very glum, feeling her Christmas day had been ruined. I managed to get through the handover and then finally said. 'The baby in cubicle two is very ill and has strict barrier nursing in place and the doctor requested quarter hourly obs.' That did it,

'QUARTER HOURLY OBS!' Sister Chang was now at the end of her tether.

'Sorry Sister, hope it gets better, happy Christmas.' I replied and left the ward. Me and the other student on duty that night then peered through the window watched her wash and scrub her hands, put on overshoes, gown, mask and gloves and go into the cubicle, we then heard a yelp and she came chasing after us down the corridor laughing her head off shouting.

'I'll kill you.' She did take it all in good spirit and fortunately let us go home to bed rather than tidy up the ward after all the mess we had made.

I had to leave the ward after Christmas and go back to school as we used to say when we were classroom based for our two weeks at the end of a placement. I did enjoy paediatrics but was definitely an adult nurse and was certain I wouldn't be doing paediatric nursing any time soon. I did much later do a spell on a Special Care Baby Unit (SCBU) as part of my midwifery training but this was never going to be a career option either. Delivering babies, well that's a different kettle of fish altogether.

Chapter 16

Casualty

It goes without saying that A&E is where a lot of the action is and it can be a high stress, adrenaline pumping job, there is an abundance of male nurses on A&E units and an abundance of superiority syndromes. In spite of this I did like working there and even considered working in A&E after training. Television programmes like Holby City and Casualty have glamorised A&E departments.

'*Hello Nurse Brookes, could you help me bring this patient back to life, and by the way what are you doing for dinner tonight?*' they are not. Having watched casualty once or twice most people might think that the A&E department is the best place in the world to work with caring doctors who seem to do everything (an absolute misnomer), including fight amongst themselves (this does happen among consultants where egos can get in the way) and have relationships with anyone within a three metre radius. I may have met one doctor like that, but the rest are certainly not any of the above.

In my experience, doctors and nurses in A&E did not usually build relationships with patients, in fact many rarely looked at the patient, they were usually interested in the presenting problem, the diagnosis and then, quick treatment before moving them on the next place.

When I worked in A&E I did learn a lot of things, we weren't allowed to stitch as students but we could do lots of other things. I mainly worked in the 'dressings' area which was more routine and less intense than the acute emergency area and I was allowed to do things rather than just watch. People came in with all sorts of cuts and bruises and were of all ages from children to older people. Weekends were always busy following nights out, sports and DIY attempts.

Summer months were also busy with burns as men who had never cooked in their lives suddenly decided to barbecue food to match the charcoal on the fire and when the fire didn't light fast enough for them they threw flammable liquids on it which tended to light up the night sky and anything in the way, including, said men. Actually I had a strange liking for dressing burns, not sure what that says about me but I did. We used to remove blisters and then apply lots of paraffin gauze, ironic that a flammable item was placed over a burn I know. This was the least adhering wound dressing available at the time although it did stick once dried out. Another common item applied was the wonderful N/A dressing, again non-adherent and then there was the outer layers of dressings and bandages, all were applied with great care as burns were very painful for patients. Silicone dressings have since taken the place of paraffin gauze and a cream containing silver called flamazine which reduces infection risk as burns are very prone to infection. There are also specialist burns units for people with really severe and life threatening burns.

One Saturday night on A&E I was on a late shift when an unconscious hells angel was brought in by his friends. They didn't know what was wrong with him, he had just collapsed they said. The doctors put up a drip and I was monitoring his observations when he woke up.

'Where the hell, What the heck!' Or some such words he was shouting as monitors and drips started flying around the place. The doctor came rushing in and tried to help me calm the man down. I was five foot nothing and seven and a half stone, this man was six foot something and huge, it was no contest he was up off the trolley dragging everything behind him, the drip stand fell over as he thrashed his arm around, the heart monitor crashed to the floor as he punched it (I don't think he liked the lights). I was trying to speak to him and explain where he was, finally the doctor called in his hells angels friends (the patient's, not the doctor's), who picked him up and put him back on the trolley and managed to stop him thrashing about. It's amazing what one will try to do when in a uniform trying to help people.

I have been in many situations at work that I would have just run away from if I was on the street but wearing that nurse's uniform comes with a responsibility to always try to assist a person no matter how they behave. Nowadays the police are called in when patients are violent to staff as A&E can be a dangerous place to work.

The man's friends confessed to the doctor that

he had been drinking heavily before becoming unconscious and so they were told to sit with him until he had slept it off while we moved on to the next person, albeit a bit shaken and with few bruises ourselves. I think the doctor got a black eye for his trouble and I got a bruised arm and a grazed knee from something hitting me.

The monitors were ruined, thousands of pounds worth of equipment, trashed in less than five minutes. I don't think the patient minded who he hit and although his friends apologised profusely, he never did. As I said there is a no tolerance policy relating to abuse in the NHS now and people are prosecuted for attacking members of staff but there are some situations where you just can't anticipate attacks.

I was recently taking the blood pressure of a seemingly harmless elderly person when a fist hit me in the mouth before I knew what was happening. Great, now I look like I've been in a domestic I thought – it's difficult to prosecute elderly people suffering from dementia and I don't always wear body armour to work.

Obviously when patients are known to be aggressive due to dementia or confusion it is easier to take precautions but often attacks come out of the blue. I don't think I have met a nurse who hasn't been hit at some stage during their career. I remember when comparing notes with Sue, Bette, Grace & Charlie towards the end of our training, we had all had a moment.

'Mr Brown ran straight into my shins in his

wheelchair and I was left with a massive bruise.' Bette explained, 'He thought he was escaping from the Japanese because he kept shouting about Nips.'

'I was removing a dressing from Mrs Bloom's abdomen post-op and she suddenly hit out with a punch, thankfully I moved quickly and ended up with a slight bruise to my arm.' Charlie shared.

'My worst one,' said Sue, 'was just after I started on the psychiatric ward, I was speaking to this patient who was very nice, he was sharing some of his experiences with me when this woman pulled my hair from behind and head butted me, it came right out of the blue and I ended up with three stitches in my head.' You win, I thought.

'For me it was when Mrs Watson came round after being unconscious and I went to reassure her where she was.' Grace said, 'then before I knew it she was out of the bed and I was on the floor with her on top of me, the other staff rescued me just in time, I was mentally scarred rather than physically and have always been a bit wary since then.'

'Mine has to be the bite.' I said. Reminiscences like this were helpful as at least we could laugh about the situations we had been in and it was somehow reassuring to know that we were not the only ones. Patients were also violent to other patients at times and a lot of supervision is required where there are a number of patients with dementia in the same place as they sometimes need protection from each other.

The ward sister on the A&E ward that I worked on was a young woman who was a great teacher, she always had time for student nurses and would try to make sure we got the best out of the placement, some of the other members of staff were the exact opposite. One staff nurse was particularly arrogant with the attitude of a Rottweiler, we called her Brutus. Whenever Brutus was on duty the students would groan and even more so if we were attached to her area. Many a student nurse ended up in tears when working on shift with her and I was determined this would not happen to me.

It was hard to report people during my training as it was more likely to kickback on the person who would be seen as a snitch and disloyal. There was more of a 'cover up' culture back then and although the good Sisters ran a tight ship and kept bullying to a minimum there were some wards where the bullying came from the top.

I did have to work with Brutus in her area on a few shifts and came close to tears as she would spend most of the shift belittling everything, it was much better if it was busy because I could try to ignore her as much as I could. What really got to us was how she spoke to patients, she was cold and uncaring and none of us could work out why she had chosen nursing for a career. We thought that she was probably deluded, that she thought she was working as a prison warden rather than a nurse.

It has been my unfortunate experience to meet a few people like this in my career, bullies basically who choose to make the lives of the weak and vulnerable as miserable as possible and for far too many years the NHS tolerated them. Perhaps the next Government reform could include rounding up the malingerers and bullies in the NHS and bringing back National Service just for them. Seriously though, there are forums now to report such behaviour. Fortunately though there are more caring people in the profession than not and most of us try to do the best we can within the constraints of an ever changing political football.

I was sad to see many people coming into the department having taken an overdose of tablets. The reasons for overdosing were many and varied. The drug of choice was often paracetamol and quite a few young people came in having taken these as an overdose. What they didn't realise was that paracetamol overdose can cause irreparable damage to the liver and they might suffer severe liver disease and early death in years to come. You might think this the least of their worries if they wanted to die anyway but many people who take an overdose are using it as a cry for help rather than really wanting to die, some obviously do want to die, many of these succeed. Paracetamol packaging was changed as a result of overdose attempts.

A&E nurses on the whole don't do 'self harm' very well, they don't sympathise with people who abuse alcohol, drug addicts or people who attempt suicide. I'm sure the stomach pumps were used a little too roughly on more than one occasion and many patients have confided in me that their treatment in A&E has not been a good experience. Unfortunately the A&E nurses are thinking that by being rough or rude that they are teaching the person a lesson and that this will prevent them behaving in this way again. Most people with self harm tendencies tend to think that they deserve to be punished and the treatment in many general hospitals just reaffirms this idea to them and while I understand A&E departments are busy with what many term as 'genuine' cases don't all human beings deserve to be cared for with a little bit of compassion?

The only benefit to coming into hospital following an overdose (other than having one's life saved) was that the patients' got to see a psychiatrist albeit for a fairly routine interview although, some, I believe were followed up. Stomach pumping was not a very nice experience and I am sure that most people who had it once would think twice before going back for more, I certainly did.

Let me explain, when me and my brother were young and we had any aches or pains my mum would give us a junior aspirin. Junior aspirins were pink and tasted very nice and so we never minded taking the tablets, in fact I liked them too much. One day when I was about seven years old I told my mum I had a headache and asked if I could have an aspirin, we were never allowed to take them without permission. Having been given permission I went into the front room cupboard where they were kept and took an aspirin, no water was necessary as they tasted so nice. Then I took another one and another and so on – whoops, by the time I had finished there weren't that many left in the bottle and I was beginning to have second thoughts about what I had done and so I went into the living room and asked my mum what would happen if a I took too many aspirin, 'you would die', she said and then I started to cry. My poor mum realised what had happened and took me straight to hospital, I can't remember whether she called an ambulance but I think she may have. On arrival at the hospital, the same Leicester Royal Infirmary that I would later work at, I was taken into a room after my mum had explained what had happened. At one point the nurse asked me rather disbelievingly why I had taken the tablets and I said that I just liked them. She looked at me suspiciously and asked me if I had tried to kill myself. I looked at her and didn't really understand what she was getting at – a suicidal seven year old? They must get them all the time. Finally the doctor came and explained that I was going to have my stomach pumped with a small tube – SMALL. It was a horrible experience and of course I was as sick as a dog. I am pleased to say I wasn't given the rough, 'time waster' treatment that adult patients can get but it was bad enough. I was kept in overnight for observation and saw the customary psychiatrist the next morning who ascertained that I was not suicidal and that I really had taken the tablets because I liked the taste – bizarre, I know but needless to say the taste never suckered me into taking them again. Not that I would have had a chance to as they were kept well and truly out of my reach forever after. My brother was only interested in what it was like to have a stomach pump, maybe he was planning on taking some too but I think I managed to dissuade him from any such thoughts with a graphic description.

We had our share of tragedies on A&E, one I always hated was patients brought in following a cardiac arrest and failed resuscitation. The scene was always one of stressful calm as everyone took their place to try to bring a person back from the dead. Sometimes it was successful but more often than not it wasn't although resuscitation techniques have improved dramatically over the years and so has the use of defibrillation to shock a heart back to life and surgical techniques and interventions are also better. Most people die because of the delay in defibrillation which is why there is a concerted effort to get as many defibrillators into the community as possible. There are still many times though when it is just not possible to bring a person round. A&E was always a bit depressing after losing someone in this way and we would sulk about, not wanting to talk about it but feeling it all the same but we were not allowed to sulk for long as there was always the next job to be done as 'hurry up nurse' was never far from our ears. There is no point becoming hardened to these horrible facts of life but equally a nurse and a doctor does have to learn to deal with the emotions that they feel and experience every day of their working lives so don't blame us if we occasionally miss the mark, most of us are human too.

I found that because people are quickly (ok not always quickly) in and out, the nurses who are attracted to work in the A&E department are those who prefer not to develop relationships with patients to put it kindly. Many are quick problem solvers (or adrenaline junkies) and like to apply a quick fix or move you on. This is not a negative as this is just the type of person that the target led environment needs but don't get admitted to A&E and expect to tell the nurse your life history. Tell them what hurts and they will decide the best way to fix it. In recent years nurse triage has been brought into A&E and the official line explains that this is so the person can be triaged in terms of importance, as if that isn't obvious when you walk through the door.

One evening I was on a late shift when a fifty year old man was brought in looking very ill to say the least and was obviously in shock. His clothes were soaking wet and covered in sand as he had apparently fallen down a pit of some sort. Controlled panic stations commenced and drips were put up with plasma products being pumped into him to try to get his blood pressure up. I was told to cut his clothes off and started near to wear the big blood stain was so that we could assess the damage. I cut off the shirt and then had to grab hold of the trolley so as not to pass out when I saw that his left arm had been completely severed at the shoulder.

'Right.' The doctor cried, get this man ready for theatre.' 'I feel sick,' I thought as, thankfully I was pushed out of the way while the more experienced nurses got him ready. I went off shift with flashbacks of that horrendous injury that stayed with me for days, even now I feel a bit queasy describing the scene.

I thought perhaps I was not cut out to be an A&E nurse after all and would leave it to the drama lovers, who were actually very good, much better than I in a crisis. In a crisis there might be choice of someone who is touchy, feely but likely to pass out still holding your arm which has been separated from your body or someone who is not that kind but can deal with the crisis and help save your arm and possibly your life? Obviously most of us would prefer the latter but with a little of the kindness, life isn't always perfect. Unfortunately the man had been lying in the wet for too long before he was found and the surgeon was unable to piece him back together again.

My A&E placement came to an end and I moved on from what had been largely an enjoyable placement.

Chapter 17

Night Nurse

If ever there was a challenge of a student nurse's stick ability and determination to finish training, it was night duty. Not only was it challenging physically because the body does not want to be up all night (except for parties), but also mentally for two reasons: night sisters and nursing auxiliaries (now health care assistants). Don't get me wrong I am not getting at N/A's as they were called, it was nothing to do with snobbery or power it was the spooky stories they scared us poor students to death with and which had us looking behind us every time we walked up a ward or down a corridor. A hospital sluice is the scariest place to be in the middle of the night. I will explain more soon but let's start with night sisters.

Every night the night Sister would do at least one round of the wards and senior students were often in charge of the wards at night but either sister or a qualified nurse would come over to do the medicine rounds with the student. When the night sister later came onto the ward, usually between midnight and one o clock in the morning, she would expect to be escorted around the ward and told every patient's name, age, diagnosis and any current treatment. There were usually forty patients on the ward and it didn't matter whether it was your first night or last, you just had to know, excuses were not acceptable. The first night was always the worst, I would listen very carefully at handover, writing all the details down and then while trying to deal with patients, drug rounds and other jobs I would be repeating every patient's name, trying to remember what was wrong with them. The best way to do this, I found was to learn them in a clockwise direction by rote because woe betide me or any of us if we didn't know by the time sister arrived.

The first time I had to do this was the worst, we had finished all our duties and were sat at the nurses' station at the entrance to the ward, the auxiliaries and junior students were chatting and having fun (in whispers of course) and I was reciting names and diagnoses in my head, dreading the ward round in case I forgot anything.

I had been told we were not allowed to use notes or torches. Even though the names of patients were on the bed frame at the foot of the bed, they couldn't be seen in the dark. I had practised trying to see them in the dark and it was very difficult without being obvious so this was a last resort as sister would pick up on it immediately. I was just starting to relax and join in the whispered conversations thinking maybe sister was going to give us a miss tonight when I heard the swing doors open at the entrance to the ward, followed by high heels on marble floor, everybody immediately stiffened and started reading through patient notes. As Sister walked onto the ward we all stood as this was the required response.

'Good morning,' she said (it was half past one) and she smiled. I knew I would like her from that moment as Sisters' rarely smiled.

'Good morning Sister,' we replied (the Walton's couldn't have done better).

'You're ok its Sister Robertson, she's nice,' whispered the N/A and I felt myself relaxing just a little.

'Right Nurse Brookes shall we do the round?' And off she went to the first bed.

'Yes sister' I muttered as I hurried up after her. It all went quite well, I introduced the sleeping patient to her and gave the diagnosis and treatment plan and then we moved on to the next bed. This was all fine until a patient on the other side of the ward called out.

'Nurse!' I wasn't sure whether I was allowed to go over or not and my colleagues must have been hiding because they were nowhere to be seen. Sister must have seen my dilemma and she crossed the ward ahead of me. I overtook her just in time to read the patient's name off the end of the bed as we were now out of order.

'Hello Mr Jones, this is Sister Jenkins,' he glanced sheepishly at sister who smiled back. 'What can I do for you?' I asked, hoping and praying that it wasn't anything too complicated.

'Would you mind moving my pillows for me, I can't seem to get comfortable and I'm frightened to move in case any of these tubes fall out.' I could have kissed him, he had a catheter, an infusion and a wound drain so I could understand his dilemma and I was only too pleased to make him comfortable as this was something I could manage. 'Thank you Sister, he said as we left to go back to the other side of the ward.' In fairness, Sister had helped. When we crossed the ward again I had totally lost my place.

'Right Nurse Brookes that was Mr Frew who has had repair of a ruptured inguinal hernia wasn't it?' she prompted kindly. I not only liked her now, I loved her. I was going to be a kind night Sister one day and I would be adored by all trainees I dreamed. This also demonstrated to me that contrary to popular opinion, Sister did listen to the information given on the ward round but how she remembered it was beyond me. The rest of the round went well and I only forgot two patient names out of forty, not bad for a first night.

'Well done Nurse Brookes, bleep me if you need me.' She said as she left the ward. Phew, I could breathe at last and my heart had stopped pounding in my chest. For the first time that night I felt relaxed and even though buzzers went off continually I was floating on air, I had passed another trial and was no longer a fledgling, for that night anyway.

Night duty always brought its share of deaths and these often took place around four o clock in the morning and so we regularly walked the wards to make sure patients were alright. If they didn't appear to be breathing we would take a closer look, no-one was going to be found dead on my watch if I could help prevent it. This was a habit that was hard to get rid of, years later I was babysitting for a friend and when she came home I told her that her ten year old son was fine and still breathing, I had checked on him regularly, she looked a little taken aback and then asked,

'Do many children die when you are babysitting?' she laughed nervously,

'Old habits die hard.' I smiled before hurriedly explaining about nursing and night duty just in case she thought I needed psychiatric help or worse.

Once the patients had been bedded down for the night, medicines had been given and night sister had been we sat around the nurses' station for a while. This is when the auxiliaries came into their own, we had just settled down trying to have a whispered conversation or do some studying when Janet suddenly hissed,

'Did you hear that?'

'What?' I replied,

'It's old Smithy again.'

'Who's old Smithy?'

'She used to be the ward sister here, she died about thirty years ago and she walks around the hospital every night.' Nervously I laughed and expressed my disbelief but by the time the conversation had ended and the buzzer went with a patient needing a bedpan I ran in and out of the empty sluice faster than an Olympic sprinter. To be fair, I never heard or saw any ghosts but this didn't make the stories any less frightening for a young and impressionable student nurse which of course encouraged the story tellers all the more. Once the ghost stories were exhausted our conversation turned to more acceptable things like boyfriends, music, books, anything else that would help to keep us awake.

Thankfully the buzzers did go off frequently and there were Kardexes to be written, sometimes the ward was on take and it would be a hive of activity all through the night, much to the dismay of poor patients trying to sleep.

We used to meet up in the canteen for a meal in the middle of the night and I have to say it was hard not to let the imagination hear footsteps on my way, after the ghost stories, while walking along those huge long corridors at night. I was always relieved if I met someone on the way (not a ghost of course) so that I could forget about the scary stories.

Sleeping during the day after a night shift was a real challenge. The world is just not geared up to daytime slumber. By the time I was on nights I was living in my wonderful top floor bedsit across the road from Charles Frears School of Nursing, most people in the house did not go to work. The house consisted of one bedsit on the ground floor, two on the first and my room on the second floor at the top of the house. Other people living in the house were Adam on the first floor, a Marxist who took his political stance very seriously, as he didn't work, he had a lot of time to study Marxism and was always looking for a political argument. His girlfriend often stayed and she too was a Marxist. I was amazed at how many women came in and out of the man who lived on the ground floor's room as he really was nothing to look at. I am not sure whether they were prostitutes or whether he was making blue movies.

One afternoon he came up to my flat and invited himself in for a cup of coffee, before long he was suggesting he was a bit bored that afternoon and would I be interested in passing the time with some sex, I was horrified, there was something in his air that was just so creepy? I was soon to be twenty and he was well in his forties so as well as the gaping hole in my sexual awareness there was a huge age gap. I wasn't sure what the ever reliable Jerry would think of this, I explained I had a steady boyfriend who was due around any minute. Casanova leered and finally left and I have to admit I never answered the door again if I heard his footsteps and I always tiptoed past his door on my way out of the house.

This wasn't the only time I was nearly seduced in the house of bedsits, one night, around two o clock in the morning there was a bang on my room door, I crawled out of bed to open the door and Adam stood there crying.

'What on earth's the matter?'

'I'M NOT HOMOSEXUAL!' he cried.

'I never said you were,' I replied, rubbing my eyes as I was half asleep. He came in and cried for several minutes and then explained,

'I was out in the park and this bloke came up to me and tried it on, he said I was homosexual. I'm not.' He protested and then he pulled me into his arms and started kissing me. I pushed him away, waking up rapidly now.

'Adam, stop, you don't need to prove anything to

me, why don't you give your girlfriend a ring and discuss it with her?'

'OK,' he muttered and like a spoiled child he left with his head down as quickly as he had come. I did wonder if perhaps he protested too much and whether he was struggling with his sexuality as many teenagers do, he was certainly a bit effeminate but that doesn't always mean anything.

I was pleased that my life was straightforward, or was it? Anyway, you can imagine that this house was not the easiest place to live when it came to trying to sleep during the day with Marxist meetings taking place on the floor below me and Casanova always hanging around waiting for the next female prey to enter his den. There were plenty of girls who continued visiting, whether they were the paid variety or whether he made pornographic movies, I never knew. What I did know, however, was that there was no room for over-tiredness, I had to keep my wits about me.

Apart from all the other activities, I loved my bedsit in the roof, I had two single beds so friends could stay over and I learned to cook on the little Baby Belling cooker that came with the territory. I didn't buy a TV on purpose, I had grown up in a house where the television was on constantly day and night and I couldn't really see what the attraction was. I loved my music and spent a fortune on my first Panasonic music centre which had a radio, record player and cassette player. Cassettes were becoming more popular in the late 1970's but records were still very much a part of the music scene. I had nearly all Elvis Presley's LPs along with many others and I was always playing music. When I was not out with friends I would stay up half the night reading or painting. Oil painting became a favourite pastime in those bedsit days.

Many nurses took sleeping tablets while they were on nights and after a couple of nights I could understand why. Bang, bang, doors would open and close, car engines outside would become louder and louder, human voices are incredibly irritating when you are trying to sleep and the sun.

'Why does the sun shine so brightly when I am on nights but it pours with rain when I am off?' I would ask Jerry. He would smile and put his arm around me, knowing I wasn't looking for a sensible answer. I would walk in the door after an eleven hour night shift and climb into bed, falling asleep almost immediately and then wake up after what felt like eight hours sleep only to look at the clock and see that it was midday and I had been asleep for about three hours. The rest of the day would be spent tossing and turning trying to drown out noise. Light and every other thing that goes on during a normal day would finally win and I would give up mid afternoon. By the time I was due to go back on shift I was ready for bed. Many a time I asked myself if I really want to keep putting my body through this permanent assault course. We would work eight nights on and four off, although the four off seemed like a lot they passed all too quickly. The first day off would be the recovery day and I went to sleep, setting the alarm to wake me at lunchtime so

I would sleep that night. Of course this would be a day when I could have slept a full eight hours during the day but no, I had to drag my tired body out of bed. The fourth day off I would try to have an afternoon nap before going onto nights again. I hated nights.

I usually met up with Jerry and friends before going on shift, I couldn't drink and so would sit in the pub drinking lemonade and after the first few nights where I felt like Mother Theresa and waxed lyrical about the self denial and satisfaction that nursing brought, the novelty wore off and sometimes I felt blooming miserable. Jerry and I would sometimes play tennis before I went onto night duty and the adrenaline surge from this often made me feel better.

I didn't change meal times around and so would have a dinner before going on shift, often a kebab or takeaway and I would have breakfast before going to sleep in the morning. The hospital canteen was open during the night and I would brave the corridors with the 'ghosts' in order to get a middle of the night snack, cup of coffee and a cigarette. It was always fun to meet up with students from my training set in the middle of the night and share experiences and a joke or two. Grace and Sue were on nights at the same time as me and Grace had fallen in love with yet another doctor, this time it was for real she would argue again, as Sue and I had lost count. Of course a month later we were picking up the pieces of Grace's broken heart again as the doctor concerned had moved on to his next conquest.

Doctors hated being called out of bed in the middle of the night to re-site intravenous cannulae and the majority of us did our best to try not to call them out. I learned quickly that if I was going to be shouted at by anyone other than a ward sister it would be from a tired and overworked Junior Houseman in the early hours but sometimes it couldn't be helped. Doctor Brian had been on the ward until about one o clock catching up with his jobs from the ward round of the morning. There would also be a list of jobs for him to do in the ward book mainly consisting of prescribing pain killers intravenous fluids for patients plus re-siting cannulae that had come out or stopped working. Finally he had gone to bed and can't have been gone more than an hour before one of the junior student's came to let me know that a patient's drip had stopped working. I went to see and tried a few of the tried and tested ways to get it going but was unable to and so I knew I had to call Dr Brian.

'Blast, he is not going to be happy.' I said to Carly, the other student. I phoned switchboard and asked if they could bleep Dr Brian. Thirty minutes later there had been no phone call and it was now around three o clock. I called switchboard again.

'Could you bleep Dr Brian please?'

'Has he not called yet?' asked the operator.

'No.' I replied.

'Ok, I will try again,' he said wearily. About ten minutes later the ward phone went.

'What is it?' asked a very tired voice.

'Sorry doctor Mrs James' drip has stopped running.

'Why didn't you tell me when I was there?' He snarled and put the phone down before I could say that it had been running at that time. It was four o clock and still no sign of Dr Brian so regrettably I knew I had to report it to night Sister. This Night Sister was old school and Dr Brian was not going to like a call from her. Sister Kennedy marched onto the ward, pleased she had someone to tell off I think from the spring in her step. She picked up the telephone.

'Bleep Dr Brian.' She commanded and then put the phone down and waited. The phone went. 'Dr Brian, this patient has now been waiting two and a half hours for you to get your lazy body out of bed, make sure you are here within the next five minutes or I will be calling Mr Hoskins,' with that, she slammed the phone down. Mr Hoskins was a brilliant but formidable surgeon who no-one would have wanted to cross, personally, I wouldn't want to cross Sister Kennedy either. Five minutes later Dr Brian appeared on the ward, he looked terrified and very sheepish,

'Sorry Sister, I didn't get to bed until really late.'

'Don't give me your excuses doctor, go and apologise to the patient and while you're at it, replace that drip.'

'Yes Sister,' he muttered and then obediently he followed the junior student to the patient's bedside where he replaced the drip. Sister Kennedy was in no hurry to go much to my dismay, she was enjoying herself too much. I wouldn't mind but she had already ruined my night by making me do the whole round anti-clockwise earlier which had thrown me out completely. Some of the meaner Sisters would know that we learned the patient's names and diagnoses clockwise from the left of the ward and they would belligerently start on the right. This meant trying to go backwards which was nigh on impossible on the first night and they well knew it and would huff and puff all the way round the ward at the tardiness of the nurse escorting them.

Finally Dr Brian finished re-siting the drip, it must have been difficult because he was gone for ages, when he came back his eyes looked incredibly red and tired, I felt sorry for him even though he had shouted at me. He was about to leave the ward when Sister said,

'You are wanted on Ward 18 doctor,' off he stumbled with a huge sigh. Sister was almost floating by now. 'Goodnight Nurse Brookes,' she chirped as she left the ward. We all looked after her, hardly able to believe how much she seemed to have enjoyed this poor young man's plight although as nurses' we got it from every side so we didn't feel sorry for him for too long.

Chapter 18

Finals

At last, we were in our final block in School, the set was now down to thirty, just as Mrs Butcher had predicted, eleven of the group had left and five had failed assessments along the way and had been encouraged to leave. My circle of friends, were all still there I'm pleased to say and we were all really excited to be approaching the final hurdle. For enrolled nurse training we had to pass a two hour multiple choice exam, having passed our Practical's and also passed written 'Case Study' assessments. It might sound easy taking a multiple choice examination but it really wasn't, I still have some of the revision practice books we had then and don't know some of the answers even now. The questions could be on anything to do with anatomy, physiology and any illness, they were tough.

When I did my RGN training a short while after, although my training was shortened by a year, I still had to pass all the Practical's again with the addition of Management, I also had to do more case studies and sit, yet another one of these multiple choice exams and also a three hour written exam. Was I a glutton for punishment?

Everything moved a little too quickly in the end, we sat finals and then we were back on the wards until results came out. Once the results came out we were in a flurry applying for jobs while working on the wards until our contracts ran out. We were never in school again and so there was no huge celebration or get together, in fact, unless we met up, we didn't know who had passed and who had failed which probably wasn't a bad thing.

Thankfully we had a bit of a party while still in School but it wasn't that good because most of us were either revising or making sure we had passed everything we needed to in order to qualify. The top and bottom of this is that I never really got to celebrate with my friends and we parted ways without much ceremony. Jerry was around of course as we were still going out then but split up soon after. Although it was a bit exciting, it was also a bit of an anti-climax, my Great Ormond Street friends had moved back to London soon after I qualified.

I was a bit busy anyway because I now had to find a job and obviously there were a lot of students looking for jobs. I was due to qualify as a State Enrolled Nurse in November 1979 and needed a job to go to. I qualified as a Registered General Nurse a few years later and then worked on a surgical ward as a Staff Nurse that was a very proud moment. I had asked Mrs Butcher at the end of my training if I should go on and do my Registered Nurse training.

'I'm not sure you would cope with the academic aspect,' she said, 'but go and prove me wrong,' she finished with a glint in her eye. I often wonder if she really meant what she had said granted I was slow to start with academically as I was lazy in terms of studying but did she really think I wouldn't be able to cope? Prove her wrong I did, going on to become a RGN then a Midwife, gain a degree, then a Masters degree and a few Post Graduate diplomas in the process.

Chapter 19

Qualified At Last

My first job was at Groby Road Hospital in Leicester on a Medical and Infectious disease ward. The ward sister was a dragon with a reputation for being impossible to work with, just my luck. Only Enrolled Nurses were employed for some reason and there were two of us who would work with or opposite Sister's shifts. There were three stand alone wards and this one was next to the one where my friend worked as a ward sister and we would meet for lunch and drinks after work.

The ward was entered through a central door and Sister's office was immediately opposite, there was a treatment room and then six cubicles either side of the main office with glass partitions meaning Sister could see all twelve cubicles from her office. There was a kitchen, bathroom and the usual sluice room on the opposite side of the building, there was also a linen cupboard, the only place we could go and hide to chat without being seen. After a short time I realised that Sister's bark was worse than her bite and although she did not do small talk she had a heart of gold under the curt exterior. My colleague and I nicknamed her 'Special' and that's what we called her whenever we talked about her. Special ruled with a rod of iron but was very loyal to her staff and incredibly protective. I think we were the only family she had. Special always spoke in clipped tones and always called me Nurse, even when I was at home. I remember the phone ringing at eight o clock one Sunday morning; I was on a late shift and had been out quite late the night before so was fast asleep.

'Hello,' I mumbled, half asleep.

'You can come in an hour later today Nurse.' The phone went dead, I was totally confused. Who was that? Then I realised it was Special, I turned over and went back to sleep. Another time a friend was staying over after another late night when the phone rang, she answered.

'Is Nurse Brookes there?'

'Who? Oh yes.' Handing me the phone, she was not impressed at being woken up so early. It was Special telling me I could go in half an hour later that day. I apologised to my friend and smiled.

'Is she mad?' My friend asked.

'No just eccentric,' I replied.

Although the ward was small in comparison to the Nightingale wards, it was still busy; a lot of patients' had to be barrier nursed because of the nature of their diseases. One of the first patient's to be admitted by me was a young gay man with Typhoid. I had never come across anyone with Typhoid before and it was not pleasant. Mr Baker had recently been to India and when he returned he noticed he was having sweating episodes and felt unwell, he was admitted to us with severe diarrhoea containing blood and a temperature of forty degrees centigrade. Initially, stool and blood samples were sent to the laboratory and the main treatment was to try to bring his temperature down and this involved tepid sponging.

I remember looking at this very young man who had obviously lost a lot of weight as he was skeletal, he had long black hair and a beard and moustache to match. He was very ill and could barely lift himself out of bed to use a commode. It must have been frightening for him as he was confined to the room and barrier nursed, he was only allowed one visitor each day and so his parents and his boyfriend took turns. They too had to learn how to put on gown, mask and gloves before entering his cubicle. Once the diagnosis was made, he was treated with antibiotics and gradually began to improve, being discharged a month later. It was always rewarding to see patients' go home, not so for Mr G.

Mr G was a homeless twenty-seven year old who was admitted after being found unable to walk in a local park. He had a severe cough and was bringing up lots of sputum from his chest, it was not nice to look at and I won't go into details. Shortly after admission he was sent for a chest x ray. Special called us into her office.

'Nurses, look at this chest x ray, you will never see another one like this in the whole of your career.' The x ray was amazing, I was no expert but I could see that instead of the normal dark areas of lungs where air was present, this was full of white patches, like cottage cheese.

'What is it Sister?' I asked.

'The worst case of tuberculosis you will ever see Nurse.' Special replied.

'Can it be treated?' He is so young, I was thinking.

'We can try, but I don't think so,' at that point the Senior Houseman walked in,

'Here is the drug chart Sister, let's get started.' Dr Jerome looked at our worried faces, 'He'll be up and around in no time,' he smiled. Special glared at him.

The next day, I was on duty when I saw Mr G collapse back on his bed, I rushed to his room, he was not breathing and there was no pulse. I called for my colleague to dial the 'Crash' team and began resuscitating. Bedlam ensued as doctors arrived but the sad outcome was that we could not get him round and he was declared dead after about an hour of all our efforts. Mr G had no known relatives and was going to be buried in what was known as a pauper's grave, an unmarked grave funded by the Council. My colleague and I wanted to go to his funeral but she was too scared to ask so I knocked at Special's door.

'Yes Nurse.'

'Sister, I was wondering if Nurse Froome and I could go to Mr G's funeral.' I stammered.

'Why?' Special asked.

'Because he will be alone with no-one who cares about him and we don't think anyone should be buried like that.'

'You may go,' Special replied and I think I saw a note of real pride in her eyes that her Nurses' cared. Special was wonderful to me after that day and became like a distant aunt, never friendly but in her way she let me in to her life. We kept in touch for years after I left the ward. Special was also nicer to my friend after that too, previously she had given her a hard time as she was relatively new to the ward.

Special was incredibly experienced, she knew the chances of that young man surviving were slim and she was absolutely right, I never saw a chest x ray like that one again, even when I worked in a Chest Hospital and saw numerous cases of TB, there was never another like that one, thankfully.

There were many other patients' I met and cared for on the ward with various chest conditions but it will always be Mr G I remember. I left the ward after about six months when I secured a place on a Cardio-thoracic course at the London Chest Hospital. I was sad to leave my mum again although she had got used to my living away and I was a bit sad to leave Special. My next adventure though was about to begin. I packed my bags and said goodbye to my beloved bedsit and boarded the train to London, this time I was going to be living in a Nursing Home.

Acknowledgements

It has taken a number of years to finally complete this book and I must give thanks to my friends Sue Dundon and Ruth Lonsdale for encouraging me in this endeavour. I am also grateful to Sue for her proofreading and comments on the final draft.

When I left school, nursing never entered my head until I made friends with a person in Norfolk who made the suggestion. I give heartfelt thanks to Gail for suggesting this as a profession. I hope that I have made a good go of it and that you are pleased with yourself and with me. I am also ever grateful to patients I have cared for both then and now, without you, I wouldn't have had the pleasure of working in the NHS for the best part of thirty nine years.